D1335266

pearl's delicious jamaican dishes

recipes from pearl bell's repertoire

VIVIEN GOLDMAN

ISLAND TRADING
NEW YORK

Art direction: Tony Wright
Design: Mo Ström
Illustrations: Karen Caldicott

First published in the United States by The Island Trading Company.
© 1992 The Island Trading Company

Book distribution: The Talman Company
150 Fifth Avenue, New York, NY 10011

Printed in Singapore.

ISBN: 1-881 047-00-8

CONTENTS

This book is dedicated to Mr. B.

Special thanks to Jenny for her invaluable help.

—Pearl

With love to my mother, Erna, who taught me how to cook.

—Vivien

*Vivien Goldman is an international intermedia woman, a Londoner.
She has written two books—one about legendary Jamaican Bob Marley—and
directed documentaries in Jamaica and Africa. One of the only things she likes to do
more than cooking is eating.*

pearl's delicious jamaican dishes

"A lot of people don't realise you can experiment with food; take nothing, and turn it into something. In Jamaica, there's enough food for everyone to feed their kids; it's just knowing how to pick up the pieces and make something."

That's Pearl Bell's pragmatic philosophy, based on thirty five years of making people happy with her cooking.

Though she's now retired and living in Florida, Pearl's a Jamaican. She's been road-testing her Caribbean cuisine internationally, catering to music heroes and regular Joes, since she committed herself to cooking at the age of 18.

Through her long association with the founder of Island Records, Chris Blackwell, Pearl has cooked for a galaxy of stars like U2, Marianne Faithfull, the B52's, and Steve Winwood. But her cooking career has taken more twists than a pretzel, from catering for the British aristocracy, to running a little roots restaurant in the middle of rural Jamaica. Each venture offered new challenges. Overcoming each obstacle by sheer inventiveness with food was Pearl's delight. Through every situation, one constant remained —all over the world, if people eat, they love Jamaican food.

She's a mother of four children, and surrogate mother to many more, as well as a professional chef. These favourite recipes from Pearl Bell's kitchen, have pleased palates so often, that they come with a lifetime satisfaction guarantee. To nourish the spirit, as well as the stomach, cook no further than these pages. A love of adventure and invention propelled Pearl from rural Jamaica to the life of a globetrotting gastronome.

The random chance you could call destiny led her to accompany a friend visiting an employment agency. Pearl was eighteen, and already a mother of six—three boys and three girls. Having left school in her early years, Pearl was conscious of her lack of formal training when, unexpectedly, she was asked whether she could cook. "I'll try," answered Pearl.

"You should never tell people all you can do," she now reflects. "They might expect you to do more than you can. I didn't think I could cook professionally —but as I started, and everything fell into place, I realised that it was good. This was something I could live on. I could make myself somebody, without being too highly educated. Knowing that you can make a living, that you don't have to do the worst work just to survive, gives you confidence."

Her initial hesitation was understandable, but unnecessary. Everything in Pearl's background had prepared her to make cooking her life's work.

When Pearl was born, the third child of twelve children, a family decision was made to send her to live with her aunt, Mrs. Rita Morgan, whose brood of six was more manageable. Presiding over her troupe of children and servants in her ample house in St. Mary, Mrs. Morgan was the cake queen of the neighbourhood.

Wednesday and Saturday baking days were a regular part of the weekly cycle. The children grew up with the delicious reassurance of knowing that the kitchen jars of home-baked cookies, puddings, and cakes, would be infinitely replenished. "Whether it was hard times or good times, there was always food about," Pearl recalls fondly.

A local riddle put it thus: "What is hell a top, hell a bottom, and alleluia in the middle?" The answer: Rita Morgan's wedding pudding.

Mrs. Morgan's baking technique provoked the infernal comparison. Hot coals would be shovelled from the fire, and placed on top of a pot lid, while the cake batter baked in a tin within, heated from beneath by the old wood-burning Dover stove. The operation entailed an elaborate deployment of person power. Each cake would take six women twenty hours to make.

Different people would be charged with beating the egg yolks, and the whites; others would grate the lime rind, and squeeze the juice. They took turns at the toughest part — creaming the dough with a wooden spoon in the big 'yabba' pot. (Intriguingly, the word "yabba" is still used by Nigeria's Yoruba tribe to mean grandmother. Thus, the slave's West African ancestry still lives in the contemporary Jamaican kitchen). Everything was fresh; the icebox needed 25 pounds of ice, and therefore wasn't in constant use. But these baking sessions were sociable events, where the cooks enjoyment of their work seemed to bake blessings into the dough.

To a contemporary urban perception, Mrs. Morgan's methods

appear alarmingly time and labour intensive — a food processor now makes those friendly night long cabals of cooks irrelevant. But counterbalancing the wearying mechanics of old-style cooking was the quality of the food available. Local farmers brought their produce to the door, and the butcher nearby supplied the fresh beef that would be lovingly spiced, and set to roast slowly in the Dover stove over Saturday night, ready to eat after church on Sunday.

The stability, the regular rhythms of that rural Jamaican life, shaped Pearl's attitude to food. "In Jamaica, almost every house has carrot juice on a Sunday, and the traditional rice and peas that you never cook without coconut. Put the "trash"(discarded remnants) from the coconut and the carrots together, add an egg, half a cup of oil, brown sugar, some baking powder and soda, mix it with flour —and if you have some fruits, throw them in as well. Then you'll have a healthy cake, not too fattening. And nothing gets thrown away! I don't care how down, or short of cash you are, there's always something you can make; and you should never throw away food."

Necessity made Pearl an inventive mother. Turning shortages into original recipes became a challenge that tickled her ingenuity; like turning the water from disintegrated overcooked potatoes into a delicious creamy drink, reminiscent of a malted milk shake (see page 126).

With Jamaican Independence imminent, the new nation began to boost the facilities for tourists in the early 1960s. Stylish resorts sprang up on the North Coast, around Pearl's Montego Bay home. With her warm, welcoming manner, and capacity for hard work, Pearl found it easy to get washing and housekeeping jobs in hotels like Tryall and Round Hill, often swapping employers according to who was paying ten shillings more that week.

Her popularity quickly led to a steady, sought after job: running the establishment of the Duke of Marlborough, who left his British stately home at Blenheim for three months a year to winter in Jamaica.

The Duke's Jamaican hideaway replicated traditional British country house living, down to the five course breakfasts with kipper and kedgeree, and cucumber sandwiches, with the crusts cut off, for tea. Conforming to cliche, the British Duke abhorred spicy food; Pearl had to grate the onions for cooking, instead of chopping them, so that their strong taste became almost imperceptible. "It was a challenge to make it less spicy, but tasting good anyhow."

Juggling the creation of four precisely timed meals a day for unpredictable and fluctuating numbers —the house held up to twenty four guests—was a challenge. Treasured faded snapshots show guests clustered, with Pearl, round a table sporting an elaborate decoration of her own creation: tiny oranges with bright green leaves spiralling up a conical tower, like a garden bower, crowning a seductive fruit selection. The smiling visitors wear bright holiday clothes; Pearl is in her formal white lacy apron and cap.

Her demure demeanour was down to discipline. "I hated that apron and cap," she recalls, with as near a flash of anger as Pearl ever shows. "It was like being in harness. We had striped uniforms for day, and white for the evening. You had to wash and starch them yourself, unless you could persuade the laundrywoman."

This period helped Pearl hone her philosophy of professional relationships. "A good employer will always keep an employee for a long time, if each respects the other. Once there is respect, it always works; without it, it never can."

In the flurry of national pride following Jamaican Independence in 1962, Montego Bay was abuzz about the Culinary and Musical Art Competition, whose finals were to be held in the capital, Kingston. Aware that many Jamaicans, like Pearl, had found employment in the tourist industry, the new government was keen to encourage local culinary skills.

The single rule of entry, that each cook's recipe must be original, was a magnet for Pearl. The preparation of the conch shellfish may be time-consuming, but Pearl was used to that, and the rubbery conch was her particular favourite. Riffling through her mental catalogue of traditional conch recipes like conch fritters, (see page 19), Pearl realised that no one had ever made a conch pie.

Pearl's prizewinning conch pie (see page 53) sums up her particular genius as a chef; her skill at bridging cultures with food. It combines the British culinary pie tradition, a recipe well learnt during three hundred years of British colonialism, with the kick of tropical heat. (See history of Jamaican food page 13).

The prize for winning the first round of the contest was Pearl's first plane ride —the first of many times her kitchen prowess would keep Pearl travelling. But she never forgot the thrill of that first bumpy flight to Kingston in a tiny bi-plane.

In the big hall of the Kingston Sheraton hotel, Pearl was awarded a silver medal for her conch pie.

As Pearl was clearing up after the show, a petite woman approached her, and asked if Pearl would like to come and work in England. Flattered, but cautious as the young mother was, it took two weeks of reflection before Pearl Bell decided to come to England.

The contrast with her old job could not have been greater. From the rigid formality—even on holiday—of the Duke of Marlborough's establishment, to the loosest of lifestyles. The new recipient of Pearl's skills was Mrs. Blackwell's only son, Christopher. With Island, his new independent record label, having hits like 'My Boy Lollipop' by Millie Small, and 'Keep On Running', by the Spencer Davis Group (featuring Stevie Winwood,) the young Jamaican was enjoying the swingingest of Sixties.

Millie was visiting London from Jamaica to promote her music, and had taken up residence in the living-room. Actors and artists, the kind who'd sit up and play bongos all night by candle light, filled the house in Phillimore Gardens, West Kensington, and needed constant nourishment. To feed the multitude of musicians, groovers, and ravers, Pearl kept a big pot of rice and peas on the stove at all times.

Cooking for musicians suited Pearl. "I could do something different. Experiment with food. With Mr. Blackwell, there was no set time for anything. I would just go along with the flow. It was only a bother if you couldn't fix something different, because you knew he wouldn't be there on time. But he's a down to earth person, who knows how to treat you like a human being."

Although Pearl and Chris Blackwell were both quite content with the arrangement, the British Immigration authorities decreed Pearl's time was up. Back to Jamaica she went.

Home again, Pearl's skills were to be stretched in further directions. She began to run a guest house. In Jamaica during the 1970s, it took some ingenuity to feed an establishment full of mostly American tourists, in their expected style. The politics of that period meant shortages in shops and supermarkets; basic commodities like rice became a rarity. Practiced as she was in making something from nothing, Pearl rose to the occasion like her perfect fish souffle (see page 56) during those five years.

Take the day the guests' insistent craving was for apple pie, when apples were nowhere to be found. Musing on possibilities in the kitchen, Pearl spotted a cho-cho (also known as a christophine, it's a pear-shaped, squash-like fruit with a single stone.) Slicing it thinly, she softened it by letting the slices stand briefly in boiling water. Seasoned and spiced fit for a festival, Pearl's cho-cho pie (see page 102) became an other sensation.

"It was difficult always being nice to all those people. But I had a way of doing it —I'd remember they were only on three weeks holiday, and smile, and laugh. Now, if I had to work full time for that person, it would be a different thing; but if you're on holiday, and you want to make a fool of yourself—make it! Because I'm not going to pay YOU any mind!"

When Pearl felt it right to set up in business for herself, she opened her own Bell's Restaurant in Duncans in the parish of Trelawney. She profited particularly from her weekly specialty, Bush Tonic—combinations of hard to find roots like the cheyney root, strongback, sarsparilla, black wiss, chewstick, coconut root, and young banana. Thoroughly washing the roots and dicing them, Pearl would boil them for two hours, then leave them to ferment into her roots tonic wine.

With her fruit punch (called Tutti Frutti, page 127, Irish Moss (a

seaweed-based drink), and Turtle Punch, made of turtle eggs, Bell's Restaurant became such a success that the landlord hiked up her rent to an unrealistic level. In 1979, Chris Blackwell asked her to work with him again, this time at his new Nassau studio, Compass Point. Pearl gladly got on a plane again.

Working for musicians once more in the relaxed Nassau environment, Pearl's life became comparatively leisurely. She had more time to experiment, have fun with food. The reaction of enthusiastic musicians, like Kool and the Gang, Grace Jones, and the B52's, seemed to indicate that good food meant better music.

"I wouldn't say I've become more sophisticated; I've just done more with food, extended the range," says Pearl. "My experiments, like making a dessert from spaghetti squash, made my cooking wider."

Ill health led to Pearl's retirement, while still in her cooking prime. However, her Florida home is constantly full of family, friends, and children. The kitchen is organised, the fridge full of mouthwatering concoctions ready to be adapted for however many people might need feeding. She may be restricted in her movement, but Pearl can still run an establishment.

"Cooking is something I really love to do; it gives me satisfaction when I see everyone really enjoy a good meal. I like to see every plate clean, and mostly," she beams modestly, "that's what happens."

Experiment with the delicious recipes in this book, and you'll be feeling the same glow as Pearl. The sparkle of the empty plates at the meal's end will reflect in the contented smiles of your family and friends. You'll all feel as warm as the Jamaican sunshine.

the History of Jamaican food

and where Pearl fits in

Pearl's cooking techniques place her squarely within the Caribbean gastronomic tradition. The story of the islands is one of a constant ebb and flow of races, each new arrival—whether forced, or voluntary—bringing its own cuisine to throw into the pot.

The original inhabitants of the island they called Xaymaca, the land of wood and water, were the Amerindian tribe of Arawaks. They were a peaceful people, who invented the hammock, and cultivated and smoked tobacco. Leaves were used to wrap fish or meat for steaming over a wood fire. Their method of roasting fish or meat on a grate suspended on four forked sticks they called a BARBACOA—the origin of our barbecue—is recalled by Pearl's Lobster Kebab (see page 50) They grew the spinach-like callalloo, pawpaw, guava, and the many tubers that are still de rigueur in current Jamaican cooking, where if there aren't at least two starch dishes on a plate, the meal is incomplete. To wash down their food, they fermented alcohol from maize or the cassava root that's still used today for the popular fried bread, bammy (see page 102.)

Their closest neighbouring tribe, the Caribs, had a particular fondness for peppers, which can be tasted today in Jamaican Pepperpot Soup (see page 26). Another Carib treat, unfortunately for the gentle Arawaks, was cannibalism; eating any Arawaks vanquished in battle, thus absorbing their attributes in the most visceral way.

The Carib/Arawak tribal wars might have sustained a regular pace of victory or defeat, resulting in digestion. But a more frightening foe landed in Jamaica: the Spanish.

When Christopher Columbus landed in Jamaica in 1492, he had lost his way. Really, he was seeking the spices of India. His wrong turning proved fatal for the inhabitants of Xaymaca (the land of wood and water), as the Arawaks called their island. It took a mere fifty years for the Spaniards to kill off every Arawak Indian.

Gastronomically, however, the Spaniards contributed enormously to Jamaica. They were responsible for importing many of the fruits for which Jamaica is now known—the sugar cane that funded the profligately wealthy plantation colonial society, lemons, limes, ginger, coconuts, naseberry, and many others. More bulky imports to transport were pigs, cattle, goats, and horses. The lard they melted from animal fat in Jamaica, was used as currency in trade with neighbouring islands.

Having worked and hunted the Arawaks out of existence, the Spanish turned to the slave trade for

labour. The unwilling arrivals from Africa's West Coast were mostly from the Fanti, Ashanti, Yoruba, and Ibo tribes. Again, the newcomers brought with them foodstuffs now considered archetypally Jamaican; ackee (see ackee and saltfish page 54) okra (see okra groove page 18) peanuts, and a variety of peas and beans (see rice and peas page 45). Breadfruit, too, came from Africa, reputedly on Captain Bligh's ship, the Bounty, in 1787.

So strong was the slaves' influence on the island's food, that even today, both Jamaican 'patois' and West African 'pidgin English' use the same word for the verb 'to eat'—"nyam".

Slaves were forbidden to cultivate cattle, but plantation owners were legally bound to supply their unpaid labour force with cod saltfish. The flesh of the cod is the fish best suited for this preparation method, and with typical ingenuity, the slaves turned the seemingly unpalatable lump of dried fish into a delicacy that's enjoyed for its own sake today (see saltfish recipes pages 51 and 54).

Slavery continued under the British. As a race, the British are scarcely noted for their food; but Pearl's recipes include versions of some classic British contributions. Check the steamed puddings and pies, quintessential British nursery food — and in direct line of descent from the Arawaks steaming their fish in leaves! Particularly tasty is the 'typically Jamaican' meat patty (see page 18), which derives from the traditional Cornish pasty that British farmworkers would take to the fields for lunch.

After slavery was dismantled in the 1860s, the need for hard physical labour didn't disappear. To substitute, the British encouraged an influx of Indian and Chinese labour. The pattern continued, with the new immigrants native dishes becoming accepted as typically Jamaican cuisine (see curry goat/lamb page 73: sweet and sour fish page 58).

The most recent, and least traumatic, infiltration of foreign food into Jamaican cookery came courtesy the American tourist invasion. Hybrid dishes, like Pearl's meat roll with barbecue sauce (see page 76), show the influence of robust American cuisine. The generous way that Jamaican cooking has integrated the cuisine of each successive wave of newcomers is typical of the island's enduring allure.

Following Pearl's basic rule— be inventive—you can cook these recipes, spice it up in your own 'stylee', and add your own essence to the mutating menu of multi-cultural Caribbean food.

Appetizers

soups

& salads

jamaican patties

This is one of the dishes whose popularity binds the West Indian diaspora together. Along with Trinidad's roti, the Jamaican patty, infinitely tastier than a mere beefburger, is the Caribbean's favourite fast food.

Ingredients:
1 lb. minced beef
1 hot pepper
1 onion
6 slices white bread
2 stalks scallions
1/2 tsp thyme
1 tsp annotto
salt and pepper
Savoury Pastry (see Extras page 108)

Soak the bread in water, while you prepare the other things. Finely chop the pepper, onion, scallion and thyme, and mix them thoroughly into the ground beef. As there's no oil involved, it's better to use a non-stick frying pan to simmer the beef until it begins to brown. Skim the fat off the meat's surface, and put it into a separate small frying pan with the annotto seeds. When the seeds have colored the oil red, add the oil back to the beef to both color and season it. Rub the soaked bread through a sieve, or whizz it through the processor, before mixing it evenly into the beef. Make the pastry (see page 108), and cut it into sizeable circles. Spoon the beef mixture into the centre of each circle, fold the edges over into the traditional patty package, and press the pastry with a fork to seal it with those classic slit marks. Bake at 350F for 20-30 minutes, till the patties are golden brown.
Serves 10-12

okra groove

Ingredients:
12 cooked okra (boiled/steamed)
1 onion
1 stalk celery
4 tomatoes/1 small tin
1 tbsp butter or marge
1/2 sweet pepper
salt and pepper

Heat the butter or marge in a skillet, and throw in the chopped onions and sliced celery and pepper, the okra, and the tomatoes. Sprinkle with salt and pepper to please yourself and your friends. In one minute's time, it's ready to serve hot.

Serves 3-4

ANY fish fritters

Here's one of Pearl's most adaptable specials—a basic fritter that can be made with any fish: shrimp, lobster, crab, kingfish, scallops, any white fish, or with Pearl's and Nathalie Delon's own favourite, the conch. The pounding needed to prepare the conch (see ingredients glossary) can be therapeutic - but remember, a classy fishery will sell conveniently cleaned, frozen conch. As is so often the case, a food processor speeds the making of this recipe right on up.

Ingredients:
6-7 large conch (2 1/2 cups ground conch)
**   or 2 lbs any fish**
1 cup flour
1 tsp salt
4 tsp baking powder
1/4 tsp baking soda
1 hot pepper
1/2 sweet pepper
1 stick celery
1 egg
2/3 cup water
1 medium onion
1/2 cup oil
salt and pepper
On the side: Seafood Sauce (see Extras page 113)

First grind the conch/fish, then the onion, celery, and pepper. Lightly beat the egg, stir it into the ground ingredients, and mix them all together. After adding salt and pepper, baking powder, baking soda, and the water, mix the whole lot into a dough. In a frying pan, heat the oil up, medium high. Then, taking one teaspoon of the dough at a time, drop them into the hot oil, and fry till they're golden brown. Turn them at that crucial crisp but not burned moment, and serve hot with Seafood Sauce (see page 113.)

Serves 3-5

roLL 'eM !

Rolling ingredients into balls is one of those fun times when cooking takes adults back to kindergarten. Here's three ball appetisers — kids from kindergarten to old age home will really have a ball rolling them up.

cHickeN bALLs

Ingredients:
1 lb ground chicken
1 egg
1 tbsp breadcrumbs
1 medium onion, finely chopped
1 tbsp parsley
1 tsp chopped sweet pepper
1/4 tsp ground sage
1 tbsp oil
salt and pepper
On the side: any sauce from the Extras section (see pages 111 to 115)
Mix everything together, and, taking a tablespoon at a time, roll the chicken mix into balls. Fry in hot oil for 8 minutes, turning once. Serve with any sauce that you fancy from the Extras section — MUSHROOM is particularly good.
Serves 3-5

Lobster balls

Ingredients:
2 lbs uncooked lobster
1/2 cup finely chopped sweet pepper
1/2 cup finely chopped celery
1/2 cup finely chopped onion
1/2 cup breadcrumbs
1 tsp flour
1 egg
2 tbsp milk
1 tsp soya sauce
3 tbsp oil
salt and pepper
On the side: Lemon Butter Sauce (see Extras page 112)

Mix everything together, and roll it all up into small balls. Deep fry until the balls are golden brown, and serve with Lemon Butter Sauce.

Serves 4-6

potato balls

Ingredients:
3 cups mashed potatoes
1/2 lb sharp cheese, e.g. cheddar
1 cup fresh breadcrumbs (or any flavored, ready-made breadcrumbs, if you prefer)
1/4 cup milk

Dice the cheese into small squares, and place each square into the middle of a tablespoon of mashed potatoes. When the cheese is all wrapped up, roll it into a ball. First dip the ball in milk, then roll it in breadcrumbs. Put the balls on a greased baking sheet into the oven, and bake at 400F for 10-15 minutes.

Serves 3-4

Sweet and Spicy Mushrooms

This dish can be a delicious vegetarian main course, with rice.

Ingredients:
1 onion
1/2 apple
1/2 sweet pepper
1 stick celery
1 stick fresh thyme
1 lb mushrooms
1/2 cup raisins
1/2 cup chopped walnuts
1 oz butter
2 tbsp curry powder
Hot cayenne pepper
salt

Coarsely chop up the onion, apple, sweet and hot peppers, celery, and thyme. Melt the butter in a saucepan, add all the chopped ingredients, then stir in the curry powder, making sure it's evenly blended. Stir in the mushrooms and raisins, cover the saucepan, and cook on a low heat for about 25 minutes. Next, add the walnuts for a further 5 minutes, and serve.

Serves 4

grilled grapefruit

Sometimes simplest is best.

Ingredients:
3 grapefruits
6 tbsp dark brown sugar
6 cherries
Slice the grapefruits in half, and remove the fibrous centre stalk. With a grapefruit knife, if you have one, or with a firm hand wielding a sharp knife, separate each segment from the dividing skin, and delicately slice the fruit away from the side of the skin. Sprinkle each half grapefruit with sugar, and top them with a cherry. Put greaseproof paper on a tray, and broil them under the grill for 10 minutes. Serve hot.
Serves 6

Ackee quiche

Ingredients:
1 onion
1 cup grated cheddar cheese
1/2 lb bacon (optional)
2 cups cooked/tinned ackees
1/2 cup finely chopped hot pepper
4 eggs
2 cups cream or milk
1/2 tsp salt
black pepper
9" pie crust (see Extras page 108)
If you're using bacon, fry it till it's crisp, then break it into small pieces, and scatter them evenly across the bottom of the pastry pie shell. Put the sliced onion, ackees, and cheese, seasoned with salt and pepper, into the shell, as well. Beat the eggs lightly with milk, then pour it smoothly over the mixture. Bake it for 15 minutes at 425F, then, turning the oven down to 300F, bake it for a further 30 minutes. Leave the quiche to cool for 5 minutes before cutting it.
Serves 4-6

creamy curried eggs

Make extra, and you can serve this as a light and spicy entree.

Ingredients:
6 poached eggs
1 cup chopped mushrooms
1 tbsp chopped onions
2 tbsp curry powder
2 cups white sauce (see Extras page 114)

Make the white sauce, then throw in the curry powder, mushrooms, and onions, and cook on a medium heat for three minutes. If you don't have a proper egg poacher, simply place the raw eggs, delicately, one by one, into boiling water, till they're cooked. Put the poached eggs into a serving dish, pour the sauce evenly all over them, and serve it up, hot and spicy.

soups

pumpkin soup

Ingredients:
6 cups water
2 lbs pumpkin
1 lb chicken or other soup bone
2 green onions
1 stick thyme
1 hot pepper
1 tsp nutmeg
salt and pepper

When the water's boiled, add the diced pumpkin, chicken or meat bones, salt and pepper. Simmer for 45 minutes. Remove the bones, then the pumpkin. Puree the pumpkin in a blender, and put it back in the soup, along with the hot pepper, green onion, thyme, and nutmeg. Simmer the soup 20 minutes more, then remove the hot pepper before serving.

Serves 6

c a l l a l o o   s o u p

If in doubt about tracking down callaloo, use spinach. They're kissing cousins (see Glossary).

Ingredients:
3 quarts water
2 lbs callaloo/spinach
1 lb any soup meat
6 okra
1 small onion
1 clove garlic
1 hot pepper
1 lb yam
1/2 lb cooked shrimp
6 medium size potatoes
1 stick thyme
salt and pepper
8 Spinners dumplings (see Extras page 109)

Boil the water, with salt and pepper. Throw in the meat, crushed garlic, thyme, chopped onion, and hot pepper. When the meat is cooked, add the callaloo/spinach and okra, boiling it for a further 5 minutes. With a slotted spoon, lift out the callaloo and okra, and chop them before blending them in a food processor. If you haven't got a blender, mash the boiled vegetables as much as possible. Replace the okra and callaloo into the pot, and add the yam, potatoes, and dumplings. Simmer for 20 minutes. One minute before serving, add the cooked shrimp to the simmering, savoury soup.

Serves 6-8

pepperpot soup

The great Jamaican classic that sets the blood racing.

Ingredients:
3 quarts water
1 lb soup bone
1 clove garlic
1/2 lb salt pork/hambone (optional)
2 lbs callaloo/spinach
6 okra
1 lb cooked shrimp
1 stalk scallion
1/4 tsp thyme
1 chili pepper
salt and pepper

Boil the water, adding the garlic, the bones, and the optional salt pork/hambone, if you're going the whole hog. Simmer the soup for 1 hour, till the meat's cooked, then add the callaloo, okra, and hot pepper, and simmer for 5 minutes more. With a slotted spoon, take out the callaloo, okra, and pepper. Throw away the pepper. Chop up the okra and callaloo, then puree it in a blender before putting it back in the soup. If you haven't got a blender, mash the vegetables up thoroughly. Simmer the soup for another 20 minutes, with the thyme and onion. One minute before serving, add the cooked shrimp.

Serves 8-10

r e d   p e A   s o u p

Ingredients:
2 quarts water
3 cups red peas (kidney beans)
1/2 lb stew beef
1 chopped onion
1 chopped scallion
1 whole chili pepper
1 tsp thyme
8 pimento seeds (allspice)
salt and pepper
Spinners Dumplings (see Extras page 109)

Simmer the beef with the peas for 2 hours. If necessary, you can set a timer to remind you when the moment has come to add the onion, scallion, chili pepper, pimento, thyme, salt and pepper, and cook for a further ten minutes. Remove the meat and have fun fishing for the pepper, which you then discard. Puree the soup in a blender, and put it back in the pot with the meat, adding the Spinners dumplings, for 10 minutes more.

o L d   t i M e   r e d   p e A   s o u p

With its root vegetables left in un-pureed chunks, this is a spicy vegetarian stew, that can be eaten as a meal on its own.

Ingredients:
As above, with the addition of —
1 quart water (making 3 quarts altogether)
1 1/2 yams
6 medium potatoes
3 medium sweet potatoes

Follow the Red Pea Soup recipe up to the moment when the onions and spices have been added. Instead of pureeing, simply toss in the peeled and diced vegetables, and cook for 20 minutes. Then it's dumpling time; they bubble for 10 minutes, and this memorable soup is served.

old time saturday soup

Ingredients:
2 quarts water
1 lb soup bone
1/2 lb pumpkin
3 carrots
1 chocho (if available)
1 large turnip
3 potatoes
1 lb. of yam
1 chili pepper
1 breadfruit (optional)
1/2 cup green beans
1 stalk scallion
1 stalk thyme

Simmer the soup bone in the water for 1 hour. Peel and dice the pumpkins, carrots, chocho, turnip, and green beans, chuck 'em all in, and simmer for 20 minutes. Next for the pot: the yam, potatoes, breadfruit, and chopped chili pepper. Keep it cooking on low heat, and 30 minutes on, remove the bone, cut off the meat, and throw it back in the soup. Season the soup with scallion, thyme, salt, and pepper, cover the pot, and let the spices steam in for the concluding 15-20 minutes.

fish tea/Light fish soup/fish head tea

A Jamaican classic - the kind of soup you can taste doing you good with every scrumptious sip.

Ingredients:
2 lbs any fresh fish/fish heads

2 quarts water
1 stick fresh thyme
1 hot pepper
1 onion
2 carrots
1 tsp lime juice
salt and pepper

Put all the ingredients into boiling water, and cook for 1 hour on medium heat. Strain in a colander, and serve it hot as a tea—or add noodles, cook for a further 15-20 minutes till they're ready, and Fish Tea becomes a Light Fish Soup. However, Pearl's favourite method of Fish Tea preparation uses only fish heads. After straining, you chill the Fish Head Tea for 2 to 3 hours before serving, and it will evolve into a thick-ish consommé that's perfect served with a slice of lime.

Serves 6-8

cream of watercress soup

This delicate green soup is just as good chilled in summer.

Ingredients:
2 large bunches of watercress
1 quart chicken stock
1/2 pint cream
1 small onion
3 tbsp cornstarch
salt and pepper

Boil the watercress with the packet of soup, in the stock for 3 minutes. After adding the salt, pepper, and onion, cook for another 3 minutes. Blend the soup in a processor until it's smooth, then replace it in the saucepan at medium heat. Mix the cornstarch and cream together, add it to the soup, simmer for 5 minutes more, then serve, with a watercress garnish.

Serves 4-6

two beans soup

Ingredients:
1/2 cup lima beans
1/2 cup green beans
2 stalks celery
4 carrots
1 onion
1 potato
1 quart water
salt and pepper

Boil the water, then add all the ingredients, and cook for 1 hour, or until the beans are soft. Puree the soup in a processor, then re-heat in the saucepan for 5 minutes before serving.

salads

Pearl's Salad Lore: Always serve the dressings on the side.

chicken and barley salad

Ingredients:
2 cups cooked barley
2 cups cooked chicken
2 large carrots
1 onion
2 celery stalks
3 hard boiled eggs
5 lettuce leaves
2/3 cups dressing of your choice (see Extras page 116)
salt and pepper

Dice the cooked chicken, peel and thinly slice the carrots, chop the celery and onions, and cut the eggs into quarters. Toss them all together with the dressing, and refrigerate for 2-3 hours. Garnish with the egg quarters, and serve on a bed of lettuce.
Serves 4

coleslaw salad

Ingredients:
4 cups finely chopped cabbage
1/4 cup finely chopped onion
1/4 cup finely chopped celery
1/4 cup finely chopped sweet pepper
1 cup shredded carrots
salt and pepper
3/4 cup mayonnaise

Mix 'em all up. Chill. Serve. Crunch. Enjoy.
Serves 3-4

CONCH SALAD

Ingredients:
6 conch
1 cucumber
3 stalks celery
1 green pepper
1/2 red pepper
3 ripe tomatoes
3 unripe tomatoes
1 small onion
1 hot pepper
juice of three lemons
salt and pepper

Prepare the conch (see Glossary page 129), finely dice all the ingredients, and mix the lot together. Cover the bowl, and let it stand for two hours. You may be tempted, but do NOT refrigerate. Serve the salad at room temperature. It's particularly good with toasted english muffins and cream cheese.
 Serves 3-4

CHICKEN AND HAM SALAD

Ingredients:
1/2 iceberg lettuce
1 cucumber
3 stalks celery
4-5 radishes
1 sweet pepper
1 onion
1 cup shredded carrot
2 large tomatoes

1 cup shredded hard cheese
1/4 lb ham
1/2 cup diced roast chicken
salt and pepper

TEAR the lettuce into small pieces. Add the DICED chicken. PEEL the cucumber, remove the seeds. CUT the peeled cucumber, and the celery, into cubes. SLICE the onion thinly. FINELY CHOP the radishes, sweet pepper, and carrots. DICE the tomatoes. GRATE the cheese. Mix 'em all up, and serve with any dressing you dig from Extras (see page 116).

Serves 3-4

Summer Salad

Ingredients:
1/2 head of lettuce
1/2 cup raisins
1 cup shredded cheese
2 apples
2 carrots
1 cup shredded cabbage
1 head escarole
1 cucumber
2 stalks celery
salt and pepper
On the side: The dressing of your choice (see Extras page 116)

Peel and chop the apples, and shred the cabbage. Slice the escarole. Peel the cucumber, and remove the seeds. Prepare all the other ingredients as above. Put them together in a big bowl, and chill in the refrigerator. Presto! A salad fit for a fine summer meal.

pulse salad

Ingredients:
2 cups cold cooked barley
1 cup finely chopped carrot
1 cup sliced raw mushrooms
1 onion
1/2 cup chopped celery
1/2 cup chopped sweet peppers
1/4 cup chopped sweet pickles
1 cup cooked green peas
salt and pepper
On the side: Garlic Dressing (see Extras page 116)
Chop the onion, and throw it in a bowl, along with the other prepared ingredients. Toss them all in the garlic dressing, and chill for 2-3 hours before serving.
Serves 3-4

rasta rice salad

The red, green and golden orange of the salad recalls the rasta colors...

Ingredients:
2 cups cooked rice
2 cups coarsely shredded carrot
2 large onions
2 medium tomatoes
On the side: Any dressing from Extras (see page 116)
Peel and chop the tomatoes, and chop the onions finely. Mix everything together, lay on a bed of lettuce and garnish with chopped parsley. Just pick a dressing, and dinner is served.
Serves 3-4

vegetarian dishes

vegetable fried rice

Ingredients:
2 cups cooked rice
2 tbsp salad oil
1/2 cup chopped onion
1/2 cup green pepper
1/2 cup chopped water chestnuts
1/2 cup sliced raw mushrooms
1/2 cup chopped celery
1 cup finely chopped carrots
2 eggs
1/4 cup soya sauce
1/2 tsp finely chopped hot pepper

Saute the onions, celery and carrots in the oil for 1 minute. Take the mixture out of the skillet, and put it into a bowl. Lightly beat the eggs, and mix them with the vegetables in the bowl. Pour the whole lot back into the skillet, and cook for 3 minutes, before adding the rice, water chestnuts, mushrooms, and the sweet and hot peppers. Stir in the soy sauce, cook for 3 minutes more, and serve piping hot.
Serves 3-4

potato casserole

A larger latke in a dish.

Ingredients:
2 lbs potatoes
1 pint milk
2 eggs
1 onion
1 cup grated hard cheese
2 tbsp butter/margarine
salt and pepper

Peel and thinly slice the potatoes, and dry them off. Slice the onions, beat the eggs, and mix everything together into a 1 1/2 quart casserole dish. Bake at 350F for 1 hour.
Serves 4

s t r i p e y   s u p p e r

Constantly feeding hungry hordes, Pearl developed an affection for the convenience of frozen mixed vegetables. However, any swift cooking vegetables, such as mushrooms or finely chopped leeks, can be used by those with a bit more time. But whichever vegetables you pick, Pearl does recommend using carrots, for their color.

Ingredients:
1 1/2 lbs. mixed veg/any combination of diced vegetables
6 slices stale wheat bread
2 onions
2 cups grated hard, sharp cheese e.g. cheddar
6 hard boiled eggs
2 cups milk
2 tbsp soya sauce
2 tbsp worcestershire sauce
1 tbsp butter
salt and pepper

Lay the slices of bread flat in the bottom of the pyrex dish, and pour the milk over them evenly till they're fully soaked. Chop the onions, slice the eggs, prepare any other vegetable you may be substituting for the frozen packet, and use everything up as you sprinkle these layers in rotation —

eggs
onions
frozen/fresh vegetables
cheese.

Melt the butter, and stir the soya and worcestershire sauces into it, along with salt and pepper. Pour it evenly over the bread and vegetables mix, and top it with the last of the grated cheese. Bake for 20 minutes at 400F.

Serves 6

rosy mash

This pink carrot and potato combo is a sweet and simple surprise.

Ingredients:
1 lb potatoes
1 lb carrots
2 ozs butter
1 dessert spoon sugar (optional)
1/4 cup milk
salt

Boil the peeled carrots and potatoes in salted water till they're soft. Strain them, and mash either with a fork, or in a processor. Add the butter, milk, and sugar if you've got a sweet tooth.
Serves 4-6

green dream

Delicate green veins of spinach marble this special rice.

Ingredients:
4 cups water
2 cups uncooked rice, white or brown
1 onion
1 bunch calalloo/spinach
1 stick celery
1 hot pepper
1/2 tsp allspice

Wash and cut the calalloo/spinach into small pieces. On a medium gas setting, cook the rice, with the chopped celery, allspice, chopped onion, pepper, and calalloo, until the liquid is absorbed and the rice is cooked.
Serves 8-10

stuffed peppers

Ingredients:
6 large green peppers
3 cups cooked mixed vegetables/quick cooking vegetable (e.g. mushrooms, zucchini)
6 hard boiled eggs
1/2 hot pepper
1/4 cup breadcrumbs
1 tbsp butter
1 cup peeled firm tomatoes
1 medium onion
1/2 cup grated cheese
salt and pepper

Prepare the peppers by slicing off their tops, and take out the seeds. Lightly pre-boil them for five minutes, so that they're not too soft for stuffing, then remove them from the pot, and drain. Mix the vegetables, tomatoes, breadcrumbs, chopped onions, butter, hot pepper, and chopped eggs together, and stuff the peppers with the new blend. Stand the stuffed peppers in a pyrex dish in 1/2" of water, and bake for 15 minutes at 350F. Take them from the oven long enough to sprinkle them with cheese, then let the topping brown for a further 3 minutes before serving.

Serves 6

vegetarian chop suey

Ingredients:
2 large carrots
1/2 lb cabbage
1 chocho (if available)
2 sticks celery
1/2 sweet pepper
15 oz can baby corn
1 large onion
4 cups bamboo shoots
1/2 cup soy sauce

Cut the carrots and chocho into very small strips and slice the onion. Shred the cabbage, in half, shred pepper and bamboo shoots, and cut the baby corn in half. Boil all the vegetables for 1 minute, drain the water off, stir in the soy sauce, and serve.

Serves 4-6

ackee terra nova

Ingredients:
2 dozen fresh ackee/2 tins ackee
1 onion
1 cup shredded cheese
1 pinch finely chopped chilli pepper
4 eggs
1 cup milk
1/2 cup cream (optional)
9" pie shell   (see Extras page 108)
salt and pepper

Heat the oven to 425F. Mix together the ackee, chilli, and sliced onion, and place them in the pie shell.

Beat the eggs with the milk and the cream, if you're using it, and pour it evenly over the mix in the pie shell. Bake for 15 minutes at 400F, then turn down the heat to 300F and bake for 30 minutes more. Leave the pie to cool for 10 minutes before slicing and serving.

Serves 5-6

bARLeY LoAf

Ingredients:
1/3 cup barley
3 cups water
4 slices of brown bread
3 cups mixed vegetables/other quick cooking vegetable e.g. mushrooms, corn
2 cups grated cheese
2 eggs
2 tomatoes
1 onion
1 tbsp butter or margarine
1/4 tsp mixed herbs
salt and pepper

Cook the barley in water for about 30 minutes, or until it's tender. Slice the onion, and saute it with the other vegetables in butter for about 1 minute. Mix everything else, except the bread, together, and stir the cooked barley into it. Tear the bread into small pieces, and evenly cover the entire bottom of the greased loaf tin. Pour the barley mixture over the bread, bake at 375F for 30 minutes, and serve.

Serves 4-6

MACARONI BEAN pudding

A filling winter meal.

Ingredients:
1 cup of any cooked beans or peas, e.g. green, kidney, or blackeye
1 cup cooked macaroni
1/2 onion
2 eggs
1/2 oz butter or margarine
2 tbsp breadcrumbs
1 cup milk
1 tbsp grated hard cheese
pinch of oregano
pinch of ground basil

Mix together the cooked beans, macaroni, oregano, basil together with one of the tablespoons of breadcrumbs. Heat the milk, and stir it together with the chopped onion, butter, and lightly beaten eggs, in another bowl. Pour the egg mixture over the macaroni mixture, and mix everything up together, then pour the lot into a greased pyrex dish. Next mix together the other tablespoon of breadcrumbs with the grated cheese, and sprinkle them evenly over the mixture in the dish. Bake at 350F for 15-20 minutes. Serves 3-4

split peas fold

Pearl's answer to the Indian lentil dish, Dhall Samba.

Ingredients:
1 cup split peas
1 clove garlic
2 cups mixed vegetables/any quick cooking vegetable e.g. mushrooms, zucchini
1 onion
1/2 hot pepper
1/2 tsp thyme

1 oz margarine
1/4 cup milk
salt

Cook the split peas with garlic and salt for 1 to 1 1/2 hours, until it's blended into a thick, creamy mash. Add the vegetables and margarine, chopped onion, thyme, and milk, then cook for 5 minutes more, and it's ready to eat.

Serves 3-4

ackee patties

Ingredients:
2 dozen fresh ackee/2 tins of ackee
2 onions
1 chilli pepper
2 tbsp breadcrumbs
1/4 tsp black pepper
1/4 cup oil
1 tbsp allspice
On the side: Savoury pastry (see Extras page108)

If you're using fresh ackees, remove the seed and all the membranes, and boil them for 20-25 miutes. If you're using tins, pour boiling water over the ackees to freshen them up. Chop the onions, and the chilli pepper, making sure that the chilli pieces are very fine. Mix them together with the ackees and breadcrumbs, and all the spices. Cut round a saucer to get the correct size pastry circles, put a dollop of ackee mixture on one half of each circle, and fold the other semi-circle of pastry across. Press the semi-circle edge with a fork to seal. Wrap them up into patties, pricking them each with a fork 3 times for air holes. Bake at 350F for 25-30 minutes.

Serves 12

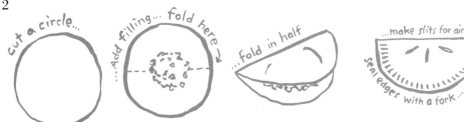

43

spicy macaroni

This recipe shows Pearl's fabulous flair with leftovers. That's not to knock making it fresh, but it's particularly handy when the folks are hungry, the fridge is full of leftovers, and the shops seem far.

Ingredients:
2 cups frozen mixed vegetables
1 onion
2 hard boiled eggs
1/2 cup cooked macaroni
1 tbsp curry powder
2 bay leaves
1 tbsp butter or margarine

Melt the butter in a saucepan, and toss in the chopped onion, curry powder, and the chopped bay leaves. Cook for 1 minute, before adding the chopped hard boiled eggs and the vegetables (don't forget, you could throw in any quick cooking fresh vegetable.) Lastly, add the macaroni, sprinkle with salt and pepper, and simmer for 1 final minute.

Serves 4

Nice spice rice

Ingredients:
2 cups hot cooked rice(brown or white)
1 onion
1/2 hot pepper
1/2 cup raisins
2 tbsp butter
1 tsp curry powder
1/4 cup chopped almond
1/4 tsp chopped ginger
salt and pepper

Throw the chopped onion, chopped hot pepper, and curry powder, into the melted butter, and cook for 2 minutes. Stir in the hot rice, almonds, raisins, and ginger, mix everything well, and serve.

Serves 4-5

cheesy cabbage

Ingredients:
1 lb cabbage
1/4 cup grated hard cheese
1 tsp paprika
A double dollop of Cheese Sauce (see Extras page 112)
Shred the cabbage, boil it in a pot of water for 3 minutes, drain it, and put it in a pyrex dish. Pour the cheese sauce over the top, sprinkle with grated cheese, and broil it for 6-7 minutes, until the cheese is crisp.
Serves 4-6

rice and peas

The Jamaican classic. When they say 'peas' in JA, they usually mean what others call kidney beans. This recipe does take time, but a pressure cooker speeds things up. And the taste is timeless...

Ingredients:
2 lbs rice
1/2 pint (blackeye) peas or (red kidney) beans
1 pint water
4 cups coconut juice
1/2 cup chopped onions
2 stalks spring onion
1 stalk thyme
1 hot chilli pepper
salt
Cook the beans/peas in a large covered pot of water for 30 minutes. Next, add the coconut juice, and cook it for 1 hour more before adding the chopped onions, finely chopped spring onions, thyme, pepper, and salt. Now put the rice in. There should be about 1" of water over the rice'n'peas/beans mixture. Bring it to the boil, then turn down low, and simmer, covered, for 20-30 minutes, until the water has boiled away, and the rice and peas is light and fluffy.
Serves 6-8

peas and beans casserole

Ingredients:
1 cup cooked blackeye peas
1 cup cooked red kidney beans
1 cup cooked sugar beans
1 cup cooked pigeon peas
1 cup cooked broad beans/butter beans
2 medium onions
1 green sweet pepper
2/3 cup chopped celery
1 chilli pepper
1 lb peeled fresh tomatoes
1 tbsp breadcrumbs
1 8oz tin tomatoes
salt and pepper
Mix 'em all up in a 2 quart casserole, bake at 375F for 1 hour, and peas be with you.
Serves 4-6

old fashioned peas pot

It's nice with rice.

Ingredients:
2 cups red kidney beans
1 onion
1 stick thyme
1 whole hot pepper
6 grains allspice

1 quart water
salt and pepper
1 lb corned beef/beef/oxtail/pork/ham (optional)
Extras: Spinners dumplings

Cook the beans/peas in water, with salt, and meat if you're using it, for 1 1/2 hours until the beans/peas are tender. Chop the onion, and add it to the pot. Add the thyme, pepper, allspice, and spinners dumplings. Cook for a further 40 minutes on a medium gas, until the stew is thick and creamy.
Serves 6-8

creamy beans

Ingredients:
4 cups cooked beans (butter/kidney beans, blackeye peas)
4 hard boiled eggs (optional)
1 onion
2 tbsp grated cheese - any kind, e.g. mozarella, cheddar
2 cups white sauce
1/2 tsp basil leaves
1/2 tsp rosemary leaves
1 hot pepper
salt and pepper
White Sauce (see Extras page 114)

Layering ingredients is always quietly satisfying. Here you spread 1 cup of beans evenly over the bottom of a deep pyrex dish, then add a layer of sliced egg and thinly sliced onion. Sprinkle the layers with the basil, rosemary, pepper, and salt, then continue layering beans, egg and onion, and spices, until all the ingredients are used up. Pour the white sauce evenly all over the dish, sprinkle with grated cheese, and bake at 375F for 20-30 minutes.
Serves 4-6

WARM SLAW

Ingredients:
4 cups shredded cabbage
1 onion
salt and pepper
 1/2 cup mayonnaise/dressing of your choice (see Extras page 116)
Blanch the shredded cabbage by pouring boiling water over it for no more than 3 seconds, before removing and straining the cabbage. Next, mix it with the sliced onion, salt and pepper. Toss with your favourite dressing, and serve warm.
Serves 4-6

cheesy yellow yam souffle

Ingredients:
2 lbs yellow yam
2 tbsp butter
1 cup milk
2 eggs
1 cup grated hard cheese
1 onion
salt and pepper
Make sure you've got a yellow yam—you'll recognise it by the golden color when cut. Boil the yellow yam until it's soft -—about 25 minutes. Mash up the soft yam with the butter and milk. Separate the egg whites and yolks, and mix the yolks with the cheese, onion, salt and pepper. Beat the egg whites until they're stiff, and fold them into the mashed yam. Bake at 400F for 25 minutes, or until it's golden brown.
Serves 4-6

seafood

Lobster kebab

Here's an ideal open air feast. Idyllic by the beach—but then, what isn't?— over an open fire, or on a concrete urban backyard, on a tiny barbecue. Or, as the Arawak Indians would say, a barbacoa. Simple though this is, it always impresses at a dinner party.

Ingredients:
2 medium lobster tails
8 large mushrooms
1 sweet pepper
2 small onions
1 medium cod
1 tbsp oil
3 tbsp soy sauce
1 tbsp lemon juice
4 tbsp butter
salt
Lemon Butter Sauce (see Extras page 112)
4 skewers

Remove the shell and skin from the lobster, wash it, and cut it into 8 pieces. Make a marinade of oil, lemon juice, soya sauce, and salt, and pour it over the lobster and mushrooms. Leave them in a bowl in the refrigerator for 20-30 minutes. Thread 1 piece each of lobster, mushroom, pepper, white fish, and onion alternately on each skewer. Broil the skewered kebabs for 5 minutes, then baste them in melted butter. Broil them for another 5-10 minutes, until they have a crispy glow. Serve with Lemon Butter Sauce. Serves 4

Saltfish and Coconut Loaf

Ingredients:
2 1/2 cups of coconut juice/juice of 1 coconut
1/2 lb salted codfish
2 small tomatoes
2 medium sweet peppers
1 cup breadcrumbs
1 chilli pepper

Soak the saltfish overnight, and remove the bones next day, if necessary (see Glossary). Crack the coconut to get at the juice, or simply open a tin of coconut juice. If you've got a hand grinder or food processor, you'll find it's a breeze to grind the fish, pepper, tomatoes, and onion together. If you haven't, chop everything as fine as possible, and mix it all up. Add the breadcrumbs and coconut juice, pour the lot into a 1 lb loaf dish, and bake at 400F for 1 hour and 10 minutes.

Serves 4-6

Fried Conch Fillet

Ingredients:
4 conch
1/2 cup flour
4 eggs
1 cup breadcrumbs/cracker crumbs
Hot Sauce, or any sauce that pleases(see Extras page 113)

Prepare the conch (see Glossary) if you're not using pre-cleaned fish. Beat the eggs in one bowl, put the flour in another, and the breadcrumbs in yet another. Dip the conch first in the flour, then in the egg, then in the breadcrumbs. Deep fry for 3-4 minutes, turning over once, until both sides are golden brown. Serve with any sauce you like from Extras.

Serves 4

coconut shrimp

Wanna wow the crowd? This'll do it. It's a cheating kind of recipe —so simple to make, so awesome to see and eat. Here's how the klutziest cook can be a gourmet chef.

Ingredients:
1 lb cleaned shrimp
2 eggs
1 cup flour
2 cups grated coconut
1/2 tsp salt
1/2 tsp pepper
1 tbsp butter/margarine
Extras: Lemon Butter Sauce

Peel and grate the coconut or simply use dessicated coconut. If you can only find sweetened coconut in the Cakes section of the store, it'll work. Sprinkle the salt and pepper evenly on the shrimp. Beat the eggs lightly in a bowl. Then line up two more bowls, and put the flour in one, and the coconut in another. Set yourself up as a small production line; dip the shrimp first in the egg, then in the flour, back in the egg again, and lastly in the coconut. If you're preparing a lot of shrimp, it's possible to coat a handful at once. Lay the shrimp out in a pyrex dish or a baking tray, top each one with a pat of butter/margarine, and bake them at 425F for 15-20 minutes, till they're brown and slightly crispy. The Lemon Butter Sauce on the side gives a delicate sweet'n'sour effect.
Serves 2-3

rich fish

Superbly simple as this fish dish is, it steams a succulent thick stock.

Ingredients:
2-3 lbs any fresh fish e.g. cod, snapper
2 tsp lime juice
3 large onions
6 ozs. butter
salt and pepper

Clean the fish, and rub the salt and pepper evenly into them. Melt about 4 ozs of the butter in a large frying pan with a lid, on medium heat. Slice the onions into rings, place the fish in the butter, and lay the onion rings over them. Pour the lime juice on top, and dot the remaining butter over the fish. Make sure the pan is properly covered — essential for the steaming process — and leave it simmering on a low heat for 30 minutes. Uncover the pan, and turn up the heat, for the last five minutes, to thicken the gravy.
Serves 4

award winning
conch pie

This is Pearl's original spicy specialty that won her the prize that took her to Britain, and began her life in food, as described in the Introduction. It's as more-ish a dish now as it was in 1962.

Ingredients:
4 conch
1 medium onion
1 stalk celery
1/2 chilli pepper
1/2 sweet pepper
2 tbsp butter or margarine
1 tbsp curry powder
2 tbsp breadcrumbs
2 tbsp conch/fish stock
1 tsp lime
Savoury pastry for a 9" pie tin (see Extras page 108)

If you're using fresh conch, prepare as described in the Glossary. After you've cleaned the conch, and freshened them by rubbing with lime and salt, boil them for 40-45 minutes until they're tender, and cut them into small pieces. Clean, chop, and fry the onions, celery, chilli peppers, sweet pepper and curry powder in butter for 3 minutes, then stir in the conch, breadcrumbs, and stock. Make the pastry, (see Extras page 108), and line the 9" pie dish with it, leaving enough aside to make the crust on top. Fill the pastry shell with the conch mixture, and bake at 350F for 35-40 minutes, until the pastry is beginning to brown.
Serves 8

island shrimp and rice

Ingredients:
1 lb shrimp
2 cups rice
3 cups water
1 tomato
1 onion
2 tbsp butter
1/4 tsp thyme
salt and pepper
parsley for decoration

Chop the onion and tomato and sauté them in butter in a saucepan on medium heat, with the thyme, salt, and pepper, for 3-5 minutes, before adding the water. Bring to the boil, add the rice, and cook gently for 15 minutes. Place the raw shrimp on top of the rice mixture, cover, and steam for 5-10 minutes. When it's cooked, mix the shrimp thoroughly into the rice. Before serving, decorate the Island Shrimp and Rice with parsley.

Serves 2-3

ackee and saltfish

The Jamaican national dish is traditionally eaten at breakfast, but be warned — once you've tasted it, you'll be ready to eat it any time. The symbolism is as magnificent as the flavor; the ackee, poisonous unless properly prepared, marries saltfish, the food of slavery, made delicious by the ingenious creativity of the transplanted Africans. Turning difficult, negative situations into something positive and constructive is the gastronomic lesson of ackee and saltfish. But eat it anyway. It's the Jamaican national dish because of the taste, not the philosophy!

Ingredients:
1 dozen fresh ackees/2 tins ackee
1/2 lb saltfish
1 large onion

1 large tomato
6 strips bacon (optional)
1/4 cup oil
black pepper

Soak the saltfish overnight, and boil it up a couple of times if necessary (see Glossary). Prepare the ackee if you're lucky enough to be in Jamaica (see Glossary,) and cook them in boiling water for 10-15 minutes. Drain well. If you're opening tins, pour boiling water over the ackee, then drain well. Fry the bacon now, if you're using it, and add the sliced onion, tomato, the ackee and flaked saltfish to the frying pan. Simmer for two minutes on a low heat, then turn it up, and cook on medium heat for about 3 minutes more. Sprinkle generously with black pepper before serving, if some of you like it hot.

Serves 4-6

conch pudding

Ingredients:
2 lbs conch
2 sticks celery
2 tomatoes
1 large onion
1 carrot
1/4 lb bacon
1/2 chilli pepper
2 dessert spoon breadcrumbs
salt and pepper
EXTRAS: Savoury Pastry

Prepare the conch (see Glossary) and cut it into 1/2" pieces. Chop the carrots, bacon, pepper, onion, tomatoes, and celery, season it all in a bowl with salt and pepper. Stir in the breadcrumbs, then the conch. Line a large pudding dish with pastry, place the mixture inside it, cover with a pastry top, and tie the bowl in a pudding cloth. Cook for about 4 hours on low heat.

fish cakes

Ingredients:
2 cups any cooked fish (leftovers are fine)
1 onion
1/2 cup breadcrumbs
3 eggs
1 tbsp oil
salt and pepper

Finely flake the fish into a bowl, and add the grated onion, 2 tbsp of the breadcrumbs, and salt and pepper as you please. Mould the mixture into flat rounded cakes in your hands. In another bowl, mix the rest of the breadcrumbs with salt and pepper. In yet another bowl, lightly beat the eggs. Dip the fish cakes first into the beaten eggs, then the breadcrumbs. Fry the fish cakes on a medium heat, turning them once. Serves 4-5

fish souffle

The anchovies give this souffle an extra kick.

Ingredients:
1 lb steamed white fish (you can use those leftovers)
4 eggs
1/4 cup butter or margarine
1/4 cup flour
1 cup milk
1 onion
2 tbsp chopped anchovies
1/4 cup fish stock
1 tbsp lemon juice
White Sauce (see Extras page 114)

Make a White Sauce (see Extras page 114) that's suitably smooth and thick. Flake the cooked white fish, grate the onion, and add them, with the chopped anchovies, to the White Sauce. Separate the whites from the yolks of the eggs. If you're not cheating by using a fish stock cube, the fish stock comes either from boiling the fish bones, or from the juice that the fish makes when steamed. Blend together the lemon juice, egg yolks, and fish stock, and fold them into the white sauce. Beat the egg whites until they crest into stiff peaks, and fold them into the sauce. Grease an 8" souffle dish, and pour in the fish mixture. Place the souffle dish in the oven, standing in a large pan/roasting tray, with 1" of hot water in the bottom. Cook at 375F for 1 hour 15 minutes, do not open the door, or change the temperature, otherwise the souffle will drop. Serve immediately.

If you want to make individual souffles, use the same method, but pour the fish mix into oven-proof custard dishes.

Serves 4-6

s e a f o o d   p l a t t e r

Laying this seafood platter out prettily is creative satisfaction in itself. It's an impressive centrepiece for a party.

Ingredients:
1/2 lb cooked shrimp
2 cups conch salad/mashed fish of your choice
2 cups cooked lobster
2 cups cooked crab meat
1/4 head iceberg lettuce
2 tomatoes
6 radishes
1 onion
6 whole sweet pickles
6 slices lemon or lime
Seafood Sauce or any sauce you like (see Extras page 113)

Lay the lettuce leaves on a large platter, placing the conch salad in the middle. In any design that pleases you, lay out the rest of the seafood around it. Garnish with the quartered tomatoes, thinly sliced onions, radishes and sweet pickles. Serve with the Seafood Sauce, or any sauce you please. This can be prepared with any kind of seafood —even tuna salad.

Serves 5-7

sweet and sour fish

Ingredients:
2 lbs any white fish
2 eggs
2 cups cornstarch
1/4 cup oil
salt and pepper
Extras: Sweet and Sour Sauce

Cut the fish into 1" to 1 1/2" pieces, then wash and dry them well. Sprinkle the fish slices with salt and pepper. Beat the eggs in a bowl, and put the cornstarch in another bowl. Dip the fish pieces first into the egg, then the cornstarch, until they're completely covered with a light layer of cornstarch. Deep fry the fish pieces into oil on medium to high heat, and cook for 8-10 minutes till the fish is lightly browned, turning once. Transfer the fish pieces to a saucepan, cover them with the Sweet and Sour Sauce, and simmer for 3 minutes before serving.
Serves 6

turtle cutlets

In Florida you'd be jailed for killing a turtle for food, but in Jamaica, the Bahamas, and the Cayman Islands, they're local delicacies. The many tastes of the turtle make it popular— different bits of the beast have the texture and flavor of chicken, beef, or pork, says Pearl.

Ingredients:
1 1/2 lbs turtle steak (about 9 cutlets)
2 eggs
2 scallions
1 pinch nutmeg
2 cups breadcrumbs
1 onion
1 chilli pepper
1 tbsp lime juice
1/2 cup parsley
salt

If the turtle is whole, cut it into cutlets, and beat them with a meat mallet until they're tender. Rub the cutlets with half the minced onion, and sprinkle them with the minced chilli pepper, and lime juice. In a bowl, mix the breadcrumbs, nutmeg, the rest of the minced onion, and the finely minced scallion. In another bowl, lightly beat the eggs. Dip the turtle cutlets first into the egg mixture, then into the breadcrumb mixture. Deep fry them for 3 minutes on each side, until they're golden brown. Before serving, decorate with slices of lime, and parsley.
Serves 3-4

e s c o v e g   f i s h

Pearl's variation on the traditional Jamaican Easter dish, Escovitch fish. Originally a fishy treat to break the Lenten fast, where flesh foods weren't eaten. The water in this dish evaporates, taking the edge off the vinegar. The vinegar keeps the onions and peppers crispy.

Ingredients:
2-3 lbs any white fish/3 small fish
1 large red pepper
1 large green pepper
2 medium onions
1 chilli pepper
2 large carrots
1/2 cup white vinegar
1/4 cup water
6 ozs butter
1 tsp pimento seeds/allspice
1/4 cup oil
salt and pepper

If the fish are small, leave them whole, otherwise, cut them in half. Whatever size they may be, wash and dry them. Sprinkle the fish with salt and pepper, and fry them in oil at medium heat. Drain them well on paper towels. Prepare all the vegetables by chopping the onions, and slicing the three kinds of pepper. Put the white vinegar, water, and butter in a saucepan on high heat for five minutes. Then add the carrots and bell peppers, and simmer on medium heat for a further three minutes. Add the onions, chilli, pimento seeds (also known as allspice) to the saucepan, and simmer for two minutes more. Don't forget to remove the pimento seeds before serving. Pour the creamy, buttery sauce over the fish, and let it sit for five before serving. Alternatively, serve the sauce on the side.
Serves 8

stuffed baked fish

Ingredients:
1 5-7 lb fish
2 cups breadcrumbs
1 large onion
1/2 sweet pepper
1 large carrot
1 tsp chopped parsley
1 small tin water chestnuts
1 cup fish stock
1/4 lb butter

Leaving the fish whole, remove the back and middle bones. Alternatively, get the fish shop person to do it for you, or buy a boned whole fish. Mix together the breadcrumbs with the chopped onion and sweet pepper, carrot, parsley, and the stock. If you're not going the simple, cheating route and using a fish stock cube, you can boil the fish bones for 10 minutes to make a stock. Stuff the fish with the mixture, and sew up every opening with a needle and thread. Hardware shops sell special fish and meat sewing kits, but if you're using an ordinary sewing needle, hold it in a flame first to sterilise it. Place the stuffed fish in a hot buttered pan, and cover it with foil. Bake at 350F for 40-50 minutes, basting with butter several times. Take out the thread before serving.

Serves 8-10

poultry

Miracle Steamed Chicken with Carrot Dumplings

Apart from its delicious fresh delicacy, the miracle of this recipe is the way the chicken steams up a soul-soothing broth, with no added water or oil. The carrots make the dumplings sweet, juicy, and light. If you're diet conscious, leave out the dumplings, take the skin off the chicken, and indulge in the totally guilt free, succulent steamed chicken.

Ingredients:
2 lbs chicken pieces
2 medium onions
1 stalk celery
1 sweet pepper
2 tsps soy sauce
salt and pepper

Carrot dumplings:

1 lb flour
2 cups grated carrots
water

Put the chopped onions, celery, and pepper, the chicken, and the soy sauce into a sauce pan. Cover tightly and cook over a low heat, letting the chicken steam for 20 minutes. Do not lift the lid. It may seem incredible, but instead of burning, as you might expect, the chicken will make the most delicate consomme stock. While it's steaming, make the dumplings. Mix the flour and carrots in a bowl with salt, and roll the dumplings by hand. You can roll them long and thin, or round, as you please; but use as little water as possible to make them stick together. Lay the dumplings all over the chicken, and cook for 20 minutes more.
Serves 4-6

coconut chicken

Like the Coconut Shrimp in the Seafood section, this is easy, impressive, and delectable. The fruity curry sauce takes the Coconut Chicken into a fragrant taste dimension.

Ingredients:
1-2 lbs boneless chicken breast, skinned
3 cups grated coconut
1 cup flour
1 tbsp worcestershire sauce
3 eggs
1 onion
2 tbsp butter or margarine
salt and pepper
Curry Sauce (see Extras page 111)

Prepare the coconut by cracking the shell, prising out the flesh, and grating it. Alternatively, simply buy some grated coconut. If all else fails, and you can't find unsweetened grated coconut, use the sweet type for making cakes that's easily available — it'll work, particularly with the curry sauce. To season the chicken, rub it thoroughly with the salt, pepper, worcestershire sauce, and grated onion. Beat the eggs in one bowl, and put the flour in another. Dip the seasoned chicken first into the eggs, then the flour, back into the egg again, and finally, into the coconut, until they're all evenly covered. Put the chicken in a pyrex dish or baking tray, and top each piece with a pat of butter. Bake on medium heat for 45 minutes, until it's golden brown. Although it looks pretty, don't let the coconut chicken get too crispy. Serve with Curry Sauce .

Serves 4-6

curry chicken

Ingredients:
3 lbs chicken parts
2 medium onions
1 apple
3 cloves garlic
2 tsp ginger
5 tbsp curry powder
3 tbsp oil
1 chilli pepper
1 tsp thyme
2 tsp marjoram
salt and pepper

Put the chopped apple, onion, crushed garlic, ginger, and curry in the oil in a frying pan, and cook for 1 minute. Add the chicken, cover the frying pan, and simmer on a low heat for 30 minutes. Spice it up with the salt, pepper, thyme, marjoram, and chopped chilli pepper. Cook for 20 minutes more until the chicken is tender.

Serves 4-6

cream of chicken curry

Ingredients:
3 lbs chicken pieces, skinned
2 medium onions
2 cloves garlic
1/2 tsp thyme
2 tbsp curry powder
1 chilli pepper
1/2 apple
1 tbsp oil
salt and pepper
Rich Thick Cream Sauce (see Extras page 113)

Chop the onions, garlic, and apple, and mix them together with the thyme, salt, and pepper in a bowl. Add the curry powder, and chicken, stirring it all well. Heat the oil in a saucepan, and add the chicken curry mixture. Cover the pan, and simmer for 25-30 minutes, until the chicken is tender. Take it out of the pan, and place the curry chicken into the serving dish. Skim all the fat from the surface with a spoon, and stir in the cream sauce. Serves 5-6.

sweet and sour chicken

Ingredients:
2 lbs boneless chicken breast, skinned
2 tbsp worcestershire sauce
2 eggs
1/2 cup flour
1 cup cornstarch
3 tbsp oil
salt and pepper
Sweet and Sour Sauce (see Extras page 114)

Cut the chicken into 2" pieces. To season it, rub the worcestershire sauce, salt and pepper, directly into the chicken. Leave it to stand for 1 hour, to allow the spices to soak in. Beat the eggs in a bowl, and mix the flour and cornstarch together in another. Dip the chicken first in the beaten eggs, then in the flour/cornstarch mixture. Heat the oil, and fry the chicken for 10 minutes, until it's golden brown. Pour the oil off, and drain the chicken on paper towels. Put the chicken back in the frying pan, and pour the Sweet and Sour Sauce all over it. Stir, and simmer for 4-5 minutes before serving.
Serves 4-5

baked mushroom chicken

Ingredients:
4 pieces boneless chicken breast, skinned
1/2 lb mushrooms
1 onion
1 tbsp worcestershire sauce
salt and pepper
Mushroom Sauce (see Extras page 115)
Season the chicken by rubbing in the salt, pepper, and worcestershire sauce. Lay the seasoned chicken in a small pyrex dish or casserole, and spread the mushrooms in an even layer over the chicken. Keep the stalks aside for the Mushroom Sauce. Make the sauce (see Extras, page 115) pour it all over the chicken, and bake at 350F for 30 minutes.
Serves 4

minced chicken

Pearl's particularly fond of that rare bird, minced chicken. Ask your friendly butcher to prepare it for you, or mince it yourself in a food processor at home. The secret: first freeze your chicken.

chicken burgers

Ingredients:
1 lb uncooked ground chicken
1 egg
1 onion
1 tbsp breadcrumbs
2 tsps worcestershire sauce
any sauce of your choice (see Extras pages 111 to 115)
Mix all the ingredients together in a bowl. Pat the ground chicken into hamburger-style rounds, then barbecue, grill, or fry until they're golden brown. Serve with any sauce from Extras.
Serves 3-4

chicken mushroom loaf

Ingredients:
2 lbs ground chicken
1 lb mushrooms
1 large onion
2 eggs
1/4 cup breadcrumbs
1 tbspn worcestershire sauce
1 tbspn pickapeppa sauce
1 tsp ground sage
salt and pepper
4 strips of bacon (optional)

Chop the mushrooms and onions, and mix all the ingredients together, and put it into a large greased loaf tin. Bake at 375F for 45 minutes. This works hot or cold. If you like, you can lay a couple of strips of bacon underneath and above the chicken mushroom loaf, for extra bacon flavor.

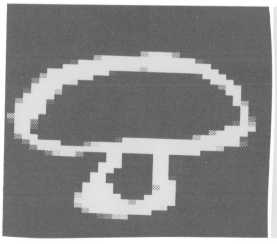 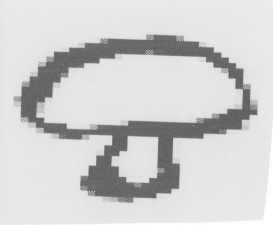

spicy chicken cakes

Ingredients:
1 lb uncooked ground chicken
1 egg
1 tbsp breadcrumbs
1 onion
1 tsp sweet parsley
1 tsp sage
1 tbsp green pepper
1 tbsp celery
2 tsps
1 dash soy sauce
1 dash pickapeppa sauce
salt and pepper

Mix all the ingredients together in a bowl, and shape into patties with your hands. Barbecue or grill for three minutes on each side, or until golden brown.
Serves 3-4

chicken stuffed peppers

Ingredients:
8 ozs minced chicken
4 medium green peppers
1 medium onion
1 cup brown or white cooked rice
6 mushrooms
1 tsp worcestershire sauce
1 oz butter
1/4 cup water
2 tbsp oil
salt and pepper

Cut the tops of the peppers, and take out the seeds. Cover the peppers with boiling water, adding a dash of salt, and cook for 2 minutes. Carefully lift the peppers out of the saucepan, and stand them upside down to drain on a paper towel. Fry the minced chicken in oil for 5-7 minutes, with the chopped onions and mushrooms. Stir in the worcestershire sauce, salt and pepper, and cook for 8 minutes more, before stirring in the rice. Stand the peppers upright in a pyrex dish or casserole, and fill them with the chicken mixture. Pour 1/4 cup of water into the casserole, and dab 1 tsp of butter on top of each stuffed pepper. Bake in the oven, uncovered, at 350F for 15 minutes.
Serves 4

t u r k e Y   r o L L

It's a festive way to exploit those Christmas or Thanksgiving turkey leftovers.

Ingredients:
3-4 cups ground cooked turkey
1/2 cup chopped onions
1 cup chopped celery
2 cups chopped mushrooms
1/4 cup chopped olives
1 sweet pepper
2 tbsp worcestershire sauce
1 tspn sage
1/2 cup sherry
1/2 cup breadcrumbs
1 can tomatoes
salt and pepper
Potato Pie Crust (see Extras page 108)

Mix all the ingredients in a large bowl, not forgetting to chop the pepper. Roll out the potato crust to a size that fits a 2 pound loaf tin. Cover the potato crust with the turkey mixture, and roll it up as if it was a swiss roll. Grease the loaf tin, before you put in the turkey roll. Bake at 350F for 15 minutes.
Serves 4-6.

stuffed roast turkey

Ingredients:
1 8-10 lb turkey
2 carrots
1 tspn thyme
2 tbsp butter
1 sweet pepper
1 large onion
2 sticks celery
1/2 lb sausage
1 tbsp worcestershire sauce
3 tbsp oil
2 tspns sage
1 1/2 cups breadcrumbs
2 cloves garlic
salt and pepper

Wash and clean the turkey well, pouring boiling water inside and out. Dry the bird, putting the giblets aside. In a bowl, mix together the chopped onion, 1 crushed garlic clove, sage, salt and pepper, and worcestershire sauce. Rub the mixture all over the turkey, both inside and out. In a frying pan, cook the giblets and sausage in butter for 1 minute. Add the chopped carrots, sweet pepper, and celery, the rest of the crushed garlic, the breadcrumbs, and the thyme to the frying pan, and stir everything up together. Stuff the turkey with the mixture. Put the turkey into a roasting pan, and cover the tin with foil. Bake for 2 1/2 hours at 350F. Take the foil off the top of the turkey, and bake for a further 30 minutes at 375F, until the turkey is golden brown.
Serves 10

Meat

cow

drunken Ham

Ingredients:
5 lb leg of ham
2 bottles beer
2 tbsp brown sugar
2 tbsp dry mustard
4 tbsp vinegar
1/4 cup cloves

Pour the beer over the ham, and put it in the oven in a baking tray, to cook for 2 hours at 350F. Take the ham out of the oven, and lift the skin right off with a fork—it should be so crisp that you could even lift it off with your bare hands. Now that the fat is exposed, take a sharp knife and cut the traditional diamond patterns into it, studding it all over with cloves. Mix together the mustard and vinegar, and rub it all over the ham. Sprinkle the ham with brown sugar, and put it back into the oven for 20 minutes at 350F. You can eat this hot or cold.

Serves 8-10

tingum's dinner

This hearty risotto is named after Pearl's favourite mongrel dog in Nassau, who was forever hovering around her kitchen, hoping for the sort of luscious leftovers that can be used for this dish.

Ingredients:
2 cups rice
3 cups boiling water
1/2 lb fillet steak
1/2 sweet pepper
salt and pepper

Cook the rice in the water. While it's cooking, broil or grill the steak (unless you're using pre-cooked leftovers). When the rice is ready, let it steam, with heat switched off, for 5 minutes. Finely chop the onion and sweet pepper, and stir it thoroughly into the rice. Dice the steak into 1/2" pieces, and stir that in, too. Heat it up, and serve.

Serves 4-6

curry goat or Lamb

Marianne Faithfull swears by the lamb — "It's delicious!"

Ingredients:
2 lbs lamb/goat
2 onions
1 large hot pepper
3 cloves garlic
1 tbsp chopped ginger
2 tsp marjoram
1 apple
6 tbsp curry powder
2 tbsp oil
1 stick thyme
salt and pepper
Cream Sauce (see Extras page 113)

Dice the lamb or goat into small pieces. Fry the chopped onions, pepper, garlic, ginger, apple, and curry powder, in the oil, on a low heat, for 1 minute. Add the lamb or goat, cover the pan, and simmer on a low heat for 20 minutes. Add the salt, pepper, marjoram, and thyme, and cook until the meat is tender. You have to keep your eye on it, and prod with a fork; it can take from 30 minutes to 1 1/2 hours, depending on how tough the meat is. It's nice to serve this dish with grated coconut, raisins, peanuts, mango chutney, or pieces of ripe banana on the side. If you want to make it creamy, simply skim any extra fat from the surface of the curry, and stir in the cream sauce from Extras.

Serves 4-6

stuffed roast beef

Ingredients:
4 lbs boneless beef, e.g. rump roast
2 large onions
1 hot pepper
2 tsp thyme
1 tbsp brown sugar
1 sweet pepper
4 cloves garlic
3 tbsp oil
1 tbsp soy sauce
1 tbsp pickapeppa sauce
salt and pepper

With a sharp knife, core 1/2" holes all over the beef. Finely chop the onion and the sweet and hot peppers, crush the garlic, and mix them all together in a bowl with the soy and pickapeppa sauces, and the thyme. Stuff the mixture into the cored holes all over the beef, and place the beef in a large roasting tin. Pour the oil all over it, and roast it in the oven for 2 hours at 350F. With this unusual approach to the traditional roast, classic roast potatoes can't be beat.

Serves 4-6

Home Made corned beef Hash

Ingredients:
1 tin corned beef
1 lb potatoes
1 onion
1/2 cup beef stock
1 tbsp cornstarch
1 tbsp butter or margarine
salt and pepper

Peel the potatoes and dice them into very small cubes. Fry them till they're golden brown, then lift them out with a slotted spoon, and drain them on paper towels. Melt the butter in a saucepan, and add the corned beef, the chopped onion, and salt and pepper. Cook it for 1 minute on medium gas, then throw in the drained fried potatoes. Mix the cornstarch with the beef stock, and stir it well in to the beef mixture. Cook for 1 minute more
before serving.

Serves 4-6

stewed beef

Ingredients:
2 lbs stewing beef
3 large carrots
6 small potatoes
3 stalks celery
1 sweet pepper
1 1/2 cups lima beans
1 tbsp oil
1 tsp thyme
2 tbsp worcestershire sauce
1/2 cup water or stock
salt and pepper
Spinners Dumplings (see Extras page 109)

Dice the beef into small cubes, and put it in the hot oil, on a low heat. Cover, and simmer for 30 minutes, stirring occasionally. Chop the carrots, celery, and pepper, and cook them with the stock and seasoning, potatoes, and lima beans, in a saucepan, for 5 minutes. When the beef has cooked for 30 minutes, add the mixture from the saucepan. Then add the Spinners Dumplings, and cook for 20 minutes more.

Serves 4-6

jagger's pepper steak

Ingredients:
4 half pound steaks of any kind
1/4 cup worcestershire sauce
2 tbsp pickapeppa sauce
1/4 cup teriyaki sauce
1 tsp soy sauce
coarsely ground black pepper

Marinate the steaks in a pan big enough to hold them all flat for at least one hour but the longer, the better (no more than 12 hours!) Never put steaks on top of each other. The steak can be barbecued/grilled, but Pearl uses a frying pan on a high heat. Wait till it's very hot and cook each side for 3 minutes if you like your steak rare, 4 minutes for medium, and 5 minutes each side for well done.

Nutty Meat roll

Since Pearl's daughter Jeminn first invented this entrée for a party, she's become one of Florida's most popular guests. Guess what hosts always ask her to bring?...

Ingredients:
1 lb ground beef
1 tbsp brown sugar
3/4 cup bar-b-que sauce
1 onion
1 cup chopped walnuts
2 cups grated cheese
salt and pepper
Savoury Pastry (see Extras page 108)

Put the onion, meat, bar-b-que sauce, brown sugar, salt and pepper, in a non-stick pan on a low heat for 5-10 minutes, until the meat is cooked. Put the chopped nuts into the meat mixture. Make the pastry, as in Extras, and roll it out till it's about 6 inches wide. Sprinkle 1 cup of cheese evenly over the pastry, then spread the meat mixture evenly over the cheese. Roll the pastry up like a jam roll, and bake it at 350F for 15 minutes. When you take it out of the oven, sprinkle the other cup of cheese over the meat roll. If it's

hot enough to melt the cheese, serve immediately. Otherwise, put the roll under the grill for 1 minute, or until the cheese has melted.
Serves 4

Shredded cabbage with bacon

Ingredients:
1 large cabbage
1/4 lb bacon
1 onion
4-5 carrots
salt and pepper

Shred the cabbage, cut the carrot into thin strips, and cut the onion into thin slices. Blanch them by pouring boiling water over them for a few seconds, then drain them well. Cut the bacon into small pieces, and fry till crisp. Remove the bacon, and drain it on a paper towel before mixing it with the cabbage. Sprinkle with salt and pepper to please your palate, and eat.
Serves 6

Crispy carrots and bacon

Ingredients:
1 1/2 lbs carrots
4 slices bacon
1 small onion
1 tbsp butter
1/2 cup chopped parsley
salt and pepper

Shred the carrots, pour boiling water over them, then drain them off. Cut the bacon into small pieces, and fry till crisp. Finely chop the onion, and sauté in a tablespoon of butter for 1 minute before adding the parsley, salt and pepper. Mix everything together in a large bowl, and serve hot or cold.
Serves 6

sweet and sour pork

Ingredients:
1 1/2 lbs lean pork
2 eggs
1 tbsp soy sauce
1 tbsp worcestershire sauce
1/2 cup flour
1 cup corn flour
salt and pepper
2 cups oil
Sweet and Sour Sauce (see Extras page 114)

Cut the pork into thin slices, and season with salt, pepper, soy sauce, and worcestershire sauce. Let it stand to soak in the flavours for 20 minutes. Meanwhile, make the Sweet and Sour sauce (see Extras.) Mix the cornflour and starch together in a bowl, and beat the eggs into another bowl. When the pork has marinated, dip the pieces first into the beaten egg, then the flour mixture. Heat the oil, and when it's good and hot, put the pork in to deep fry until golden brown. Take the pork out of the oil, and drain on a paper towel. Put the deep fried pork into a saucepan with the sweet and sour sauce, and simmer for 2 minutes before serving. Alternatively, you can serve the sauce on the side.

Serves 4-6

desserts

"Why do I list so many desserts? Because I have a sweet tooth," says Pearl Bell. The steamed puddings may remind you of English traditional nursery fare, but such sweetmeats can be found in Jamaican recipes from the 18th century. What pleased plantation palates still tickles tummies today.

bananas

...the fortune of Jamaica...

banana flambé

Turn the lights down low, then deposit this before friends with a flourish. The flames should be dramatic. Tia Maria is the Jamaican national coffee liqueur. Go with the alcohol, rather than the straight black coffee, if you desire a more relaxed and uninhibited soiree. Beause you can't go wrong with this dessert, it's the perfect impressive finale for that special dinner party.

Ingredients:
6 ripe bananas
2 tbsp butter
4 tbsp brown sugar/honey
1 tbsp cinnamon
1/2 cup Tia Maria
 or 1/2 cup strong black coffee
1/2 cup rum
Coconut Cream(see Extras page 118)

Melt the sugar and butter together in a large skillet, on low heat, and add the peeled bananas. Sprinkle them evenly with cinnamon. Mix the Tia Maria or coffee with half the rum, 1/4 cup, and pour it all over the bananas. Turning the bananas once on each side, cook them on medium heat for 10 minutes on each side. Before serving, pour the remaining 1/4 cup of rum over the bananas, and set it alight. To dampen the flames—after they've had their big impact, of course—have some coconut cream ready on the side.

baked banana supreme

Ingredients:
12 baked bananas
12 tsp syrup
1/4 cup hot water
1 tbsp gelatine
6 oz pack strawberry jello
1 pint whipped cream
Coconut Cream (see Extras page 118)

Bake the bananas at 400 F for 15-20 minutes, until they're soft. Dissolve the gelatine in warm water. When the bananas are baked, blend them with the liquid gelatine. Prepare the Coconut Cream, and the jello. In medium sized sundae cups, alternate layers of jello, coconut cream, and the banana mixture, and refrigerate for 1 hour. Garnish with whipped cream before serving.

baked banana and lime delight

Ingredients:
2 dozen well ripe bananas
1 1/2 cups dark brown sugar
2 tsp. cinnamon
2 limes

Peel the bananas, and arrange them in a baking dish. Sprinkle them evenly with the cinnamon, and the juice of one of the limes. Slice the remaining lime, and arrange the slices around the bananas. Sprinkle the lot with brown sugar, and bake at 350 F for 1 hour. Leave the bananas to stand for 15 minutes before serving. You can serve it with any kind of cream from Extras. This is also great eaten cold—but there probably won't be any left.

sweet steamed bananas

Her's a dessert that's a direct descendant of Arawak Indian tribal fare. In Jamaica, they call it "Dukunu", wrapping the puréed banana mixture in a "quailed" green banana leaf that has been softened over a fire. We generally tend to go for the less organic, but more convenient, aluminum foil. Start making this in advance of the other courses. By the time you've finished your entrée, the pudding will be suitably steamed.

Ingredients:
12 green bananas
1 1/2 cups flour
1/2 cup raisins
1/2 tsp nutmeg
1 tsp vanilla
1/4 tsp salt
1/2 tsp cinnamon
2 cups sugar
1/2 cup coconut juice/coconut milk (see Extras page 118)
Ice Cream or Coconut Cream (optional)

Peel, wash, and purée the bananas in a food processor, then add the flour. In a separate bowl, combine the coconut juice, sugar, raisins, vanilla, nutmeg, and salt. Mix the sweet and spicy coconut liquid in with the banana and flour to make a 'dough'. Wrap it up in a big piece of aluminum foil in any shape you want—Pearl favors a cube—and tie the foil with string. Boil it for around 1 1/2 hours, and unwrap it before your intrigued and impressed guests. This can be served with any sweet dressing from ice cream to coconut cream and can be eaten hot or cold.

fruit

summer fruit platter

This lavish cornucopia of tropical fruits, this profusion of plenty, is great by design. Entertain yourself and yor co-eaters by arranging the fruit as pleasingly as possible. All ingredients are flexible and can be replaced with seasonal fruits of your choice.

Ingredients:
2 ripe bananas
3 medium oranges
1 grapefruit
4 slices watermelon
1 pint strawberries
4 slices pineapple
1 large mango
4 slices honeydew melon
1 cup grated coconut
1/2 cup icing sugar

Heap the grated coconut up in the centre of a large serving platter. Peel the oranges and grapefruit, and split them into segments. Peel the mango, pineapple, honeydew melon, and slice them up. Wash the strawberries, and remove their top leaves. Now lay the fruits out around the coconut in a pattern that delights, and chill before serving with icing sugar on the side.

Mellow and fine pineapple

Ingredients:
6 ozs butter
1 lb dark brown sugar
2 fresh pineapples
1/2 cup brandy
Optional: Coconut Cream (see Extras page 118)

Melt the butter in a saucepan and add the sugar. Peel and slice the pineapple, making sure you don't lose too much juice. Put the pineapple pieces into a greased baking dish, and pour the butter/sugar liquid evenly all over it. Bake for 30 minutes at 350 F. Take the pineapple out of the oven, and pour 1/2 cup of brandy evenly all over it. Bake for another 20 minutes at 350 F, to allow the pineapple to absorb the brandy and color the pineapple. Let the pineapple cool down just slightly for five minutes before serving it, still warm, with Coconut Cream, or ice cream.

Strawberry Mousse

Ingredients:
16 ozs strawberries
1 1/2 tsp lemon juice
2 tbsp Grand Marnier (optional)
4 ozs icing sugar
1 pint double cream
3 egg whites

Remove the leaves from the top of the strawberries, and put almost all of them into the blender with the lemon juice, sugar, and the Grand Marnier, if you're feeling frisky. Don't forget to save a handful of strawberries to use as a garnish later. Whip just 2/3 of your pint of double cream, until it's stiff. In another bowl, beat the egg whites until they start to peak. Fold the beaten egg and the cream in together, then fold in the blended strawberries. Put the mixture into a dish, and chill the mousse well in the fridge, for about 1 hour. Before serving, decorate the mousse with the whole strawberries and the remaining whipped cream.

Steamed Puddings

Knotting the cheesecloth round the rim of a pudding basin and leaving it to steam for hours is a gratifyingly leisurely and tactile form of cooking. If you start to steam a pudding before preparing the rest of a meal, it'll be ready just when everyone's digested their main course. No dessert is more warming and soothing.

Health and Wealth Pudding

Ingredients:
4 ozs wheatbread breadcrumbs

4 ozs whole wheat flour
2 eggs
2 ozs currants
2 tbsp treacle
1 tsp baking powder
2 ozs brown sugar
3 ozs butter/margarine(or lard/shortening/suet)
1/4 tsp nutmeg
juice and rind of 1 lemon

Thoroughly mix all the ingredients into a pudding basin. Knot a cheesecloth round the rim, and gently steam for 2 hours in a saucepan full of boiling water. Can be eaten hot or cold.

chocolate pudding

Although suitable for stale leftover bread, fresh breadcrumbs will work fine.

Ingredients:
2 cups breadcrumbs
2 ozs butter/margarine
1 cup milk
4 tbsp cocoa
3/4 cup brown sugar
1 egg
1 tsp baking powder
a dash of cinnamon and nutmeg
1/2 tsp vanilla
pinch of salt
Optional: 1/2 pint whipped cream

In a bowl, mix together the breadcrumbs, sugar, salt, vanilla, cinnamon, nutmeg, and baking powder. Fold in the soft butter or margarine. Warm the milk in a saucepan, and mix in the cocoa powder. Lightly beat the eggs, and fold them into the bowl. Pour the whole mixture into a pudding basin, knot a cheesecloth round the rim, and boil in a saucepan of water for about 2 hours. This can be eaten cold, if you can wait that long. Whipped cream or ice cream is fabulous served on the side.

cHrIStMaS puddINg

This mother of all steamed puddings can be prepared a couple of days ahead of time, and allowed to sit until the big day.

Ingredients:
1 1/2 cups butter/margarine(or shortening/suet)
1 1/2 cups brown sugar
1 1/4 cups flour
2 cups breadcrumbs
3/4 cups milk
4 eggs
1/2 tsp baking soda
1 cup raisins
1 cup chopped cherries
1 cup currants
3 cups soaked dried fruit
1 cup chopped dates
1/4 cup chopped nuts
1/2 tsp nutmeg
1/4 tsp cinnamon
1/4 tsp mixed spices
1/2 cup wine/brandy/rum
1/4 cup browning
Rum Butter Sauce (see Extras page 112)

In a large bowl, mix together the flour, sugar, and butter (or alternative), and all the different fruits and nuts. In a separate bowl, pour the milk over the breadcrumbs, and then add them in to the flour and fruit mix. Next add the spices, and the browning, and stir well in. In a separate bowl, beat the eggs, then fold them in to the mix. Add the brandy, rum, or wine. In a teaspoon of warm water, dissolve the baking soda, then throw that in to the pudding mix. Grease a big pudding dish, and line it with wax paper, to ensure easy removal of the pud when it's ready. Pour the whole mixture into the lined pudding dish, tie it tightly with a cheesecloth around the rim, steam in a large saucepan of hot water for 5 hours, and store until needed. Pearl knows of Christmas pudding that was perfect after having been kept for 2 years! Without a freezer or fridge! The pudding must be covered securely, airtight. Before serving, steam for another 2 hours, and serve with Rum Butter Sauce on the side.

eggless plum pudding

Ingredients:
1 1/4 cups sour milk
1/2 cup treacle
1 cup enriched flour
1/3 tsp salt
1 1/2 cups stale breadcrumbs
1 cup butter/margarine (or lard/suet)
2 tbsp brown sugar
1 tbsp boiling water
1 tsp baking soda
1 cup raisins
1 cup currants
1 cup chopped prunes
1 cup chopped cherries
1/2 cup mixed lemon and lime peel
1/2 cup chopped figs
1/2 cup chopped dates
1 cup white rum
1 cup port wine
1 tsp vanilla
1/4 tsp mixed spice

Mix and sift together the flour, salt, spices, breadcrumbs, butter (or alternative), sugar, and dried fruits. Mix together the syrup and milk while warming in a saucepan, and beat well. Pour the liquid mixture evenly over the dry ingredients, dissolve the baking soda in one tablespoon of warm water, and mix it all up well. Now stir in the white rum, port wine and vanilla. Fill a buttered steaming bowl with the mixture, tie it with a cheesecloth, and steam for 2 hours.

steamed carrots and apple pudding

Ingredients:
1 cup breadcrumbs
1/2 cup flour
1/4 lb butter
1 cup brown sugar
3 eggs
1 tsp nutmeg
1 tsp cinnamon
1 1/2 cups chopped apple
1 1/2 cups shredded carrots
3/4 cups chopped walnuts
1/2 cup sultanas/raisins
1 tsp baking powder
pinch of baking soda

Beat together the butter, sugar, and eggs. Throw in everything else—the apple, carrots, nuts, sultanas, spices, flour, breadcrumbs, baking powder, and baking soda—and mix in a pudding bowl. Tie a cheesecloth round the rim, and steam in a saucepan of boiling water for 2 hours.

pumpkin pudding

Ingredients:
2 cups shredded pumpkin
1/4 lb butter
1/4 lb sugar
1/4 lb flour
3 eggs
1/2 cup nuts and raisins (optional)
1 tsp ground ginger
1/2 tsp cinnamon

1/8 tsp ground cloves
1/2 tsp vanilla
1 tsp baking powder
1/2 tsp lemon juice
1/2 tsp lemon rind
a pinch of salt

Cream together the butter and sugar in a bowl, or a food processor. Add the eggs, and beat it all together until it's creamy. Using the same bowl, fold in the flour, then mix in the shredded pumpkin, lemon juice and rind, salt, and baking powder, and all the spices. Now's the time for the nuts and raisins, if you're using them. Bake in an 8" pyrex dish or similar receptacle for 30 minutes at 375 F. Let the pudding cool down before serving it, to make slicing easier.

sweet potato pudding

Ingredients:
2 lbs sweet potatoes
1 tbsp butter/margarine
1 cup flour
1 cup soaked dried fruits/currants/raisins (see 'pudding' introduction)
1/4 cup rum
1/2 cup dark brown sugar
1 tbsp vanilla
1/2 tsp nutmeg
1 tsp cinnamon
1/4 tsp salt
coconut juice

Stir the sugar into the coconut juice. Mix the butter, vanilla, nutmeg, salt, and cinnamon together with the butter and the rum. Peel the sweet potatoes and grate them in a food processor, then stir in the soaked dried fruit. Pour it all into a greased baking dish, and bake for 90 minutes at 375 F. This is good sliced cold, too.

plantain pudding

Ingredients:
4 well ripe plantains
2 cups milk
1 cup sugar
2 tbsp butter
3 eggs
2 tbsp flour
1/4 tsp nutmeg
1/2 tsp vanilla
1/4 cup rum
1/2 cup chopped mixed nuts
1/2 cup raisins

Cream the plantains, butter, and sugar, together in a bowl, or in a food processor. Add the eggs one at a time, and mix well in. Mix together the flour, nuts, raisins, nutmeg, and vanilla, and mix the rum and milk separately. Mix together the flour mix into the plantains, then stir in some rum and milk. Alternate adding the flour and milk mixtures into the plantain, slowly, until everything's used up. Then pour everything into a greased baking dish about two inches high, and bake for 45 minutes at 375 F, until the pudding is golden brown. Let it cool before serving.

cornmeal pudding

Ingredients:
2 cups cornmeal
1 cup flour
1 tbsp butter
2 cups sugar
2 eggs
1/2 tsp nutmeg
1 tsp cinnamon
1 tsp allspice

pinch of salt
2 tsp vanilla
3 1/2 cups coconut juice

Mix all of the dry ingredients—the cornmeal, the flour, and spices—well together in a bowl. In a separate bowl, mix the butter, vanilla, coconut juice, and lightly beaten eggs together. Pour the coconut/egg liquid over the dry ingredients, mix well, and pour it into a greased, two quart baking dish or tin. Bake for 2 hours at 375 F. until it's golden brown. Let this pudding cool for 15 minutes before serving.

cornmeal and sweet potato pudding

Ingredients:
2 cups cornmeal
2 cups grated sweet potato (1 lb sweet potato)
3 1/2 cups sugar
5 cups coconut juice
2 tbsp flour
1 tbsp butter
2 tsp vanilla
1/2 tsp nutmeg
1 tsp cinnamon
1/2 tsp salt
1 cup dried mixed fruit

Peel the sweet potato and grate (in a food processor, if possible). Put the sweet potato and mixed fruit into a big bowl, and add the flour and cornmeal, mixing it all up together. Now add the coconut juice, the sugar, vanilla, nutmeg, cinnamon, butter, and salt, and mix that all in. Pour into a two quart baking pan or oven-proof dish and bake for 1 1/2 hours at 375 F., until it's golden brown. Allow to cool before serving.

apple bread pudding

A scrumptious apple sandwich omelette, that looks like a toasted flying saucer landed in your frying pan.

Ingredients:
1 lb cooking apples
4 ozs breadcrumbs
2 large eggs
1/2 tsp cinnamon
1 tbsp milk
1 oz sugar
2 ozs raisins
1 oz butter or margarine
1 tbsp oil
1 tbsp caster or icing sugar (optional)
1 pint whipped cream
Extras: any sweet cream, custard, or ice cream

In a bowl, lightly beat together the milk and eggs. Peel and grate the apples, and add them to the bowl along with the breadcrumbs, cinnamon, sugar and sultanas. Use a fork to mix everything together into a dough. In a frying pan, heat the oil and butter, and turn the dough into the pan. Put a lid on the pan, and cook the pudding gently for 10-15 minutes, making sure that the underside of the pud doesn't burn. When the underside is cooked, slide it out onto an oiled plate, then slide it back in, with the uncooked side down, and carry on cooking it gently for another 10-15 minutes. When it's done, sprinkle it with caster sugar, if you've got a sweet tooth like Pearl, and serve with whipped cream or ice cream.
Serves 4-6.

cakes and other baked treats

yoghurt cake

Ingredients:
2 ozs butter
1 egg
1 cup flour
1 tsp baking powder
3/4 cup any yoghurt
Mix everything well together, and bake in a tin at 375F. for 30 minutes, until it's golden brown. Leave it to cool before serving.

baked apple bread sandwich

Ingredients:
6 slices bread
6 cups grated apple (2 lbs apples)
2 eggs
2 ozs butter
1 cup sugar/honey
1 tsp cinnamon
1/2 cup raisins
1 cup orange juice
Peel and grate the apples. Butter the bread and make sandwiches with the apples and raisins. Lay the sandwiches in a dish. Beat the eggs in a bowl, add the sugar, orange juice, and spices, and pour them evenly over the bread. Leave it to soak for 10-15 minutes, then sprinkle with brown sugar and bake at 375F. for 30 minutes.

sponge cake

Ingredients:
4 ozs margarine
1/4 lb sugar
2 eggs
1/4 lb self-raising flour
1 level tsp baking powder
Extras: Filling of your choice

Mix everything together in a bowl, and bake at 350F. for 30 minutes, until golden brown. Cool before serving. Slice across the middle to put in filling of your choice.

carrot cake

Ingredients:
1 1/2 cups grated carrots
1/2 cup butter
1 cup sugar
4 eggs
1 cup chopped mixed nuts
1 cup chopped walnuts
2 tsp vanilla
1/4 tsp cinammon
1/2 tsp nutmeg
1/2 lb flour
3 tsp baking powder
1/8 tsp baking soda

Cream the sugar and butter together, and add the eggs one at a time, beating them well in. Peel and grate the carrots, and add them to the vanilla, and all the other dry ingredients—nuts, walnuts, spices, baking powder and soda. Mix thoroughly together, and pour into a greased baking tin. Bake at 350F. for 1 hour and 10 minutes. Eat hot or cold.

Honey Honey cake

Ingredients:
1 lb self-raising flour
1 cup honey
4 eggs
1/2 cup milk
1/2 cup butter
1/4 tsp ground cloves
1/4 cup ground almonds
2 tsp baking powder
1 tsp grated lemon rind
1 cup brown sugar
1/4 tsp mace
Honey Butter Cream (see Extras page 117)

Beat the butter and sugar until it's creamy. Then beat in the eggs, one at a time, the flour, and the milk, until they're all creamed in. Stir in the almonds and honey, making sure to mix very well. Bake the mixture at 350F. for 25 minutes in two greased 8" layer cake tins. Cool the cakes down, fill them with Honey Butter Cream from Extras, and sandwich together. Spread more cream over the top of the cake as icing.

tea cakes

This recipe makes 12 cupcakes.
Ingredients:
6 ozs self-raising flour
1 tsp baking powder
4 ozs butter
4 ozs sugar
2 eggs
1/2 cup raisins (optional)
pinch of salt

Sift the flour and baking powder together with a pinch of salt. Cream the softened butter together with the sugar and eggs, and add it in to the flour mixture, blending everything thoroughly together, in a food processor if you have one. Add the raisins now, if you're going to. Pour the mixture into lined cupcake tins, and bake for 20 minutes at 400F. Cool before serving.

pumpkin tea cake

Ingredients:
2 cups shredded pumpkin (1/2 lb pumpkin)
1/4 lb butter
1/4 lb sugar
1/2 lb flour
3 eggs
1/2 cup raisins
1/2 cup chopped nuts
2 tsp ginger
1/2 tsp cinnamon
dash of cloves
1/2 tsp vanilla
1/2 tsp lemon juice
1/2 tsp lemon rind
1/2 tsp baking powder
pinch of salt

Peel the pumpkin, remove the seeds, and shred it in a food processor (if available). Cream the butter and sugar together. Add the eggs one at a time, then the shredded pumpkin, and all the spices. Now add in the flour, baking powder, and salt. Next, put in the lemon rind and juice, the nuts, and raisins and fold everything in together. Bake at 375F. for 30 minutes, and serve either hot or cold.

eggless butterless cake

Ingredients:
3 cups flour
1 cup sugar
1/2 cup shortening/vegetable oil
1 tsp. lime juice

1 cup orange juice
1 cup boiling water
1 tbspn orange rind
1 tsp baking powder
1 tsp baking soda
1/2 tsp vanilla
1/2 tsp nutmeg

Mix together the flour, baking powder, baking soda, nutmeg, and salt. Cream together the sugar and shortening separately. Add the orange and lime juice, then stir in the boiling water and orange rind. Combine the two mixtures, bake at 350F. for 40-50 minutes, and serve either hot or cold.

ſ p o n g e   ſ a n d w i c h   c a k e

Ingredients:
1/4 lb butter
1/4 lb sugar
2 large /3 small eggs
1/4 lb self-raising flour
1 tbsp cold water
1/2 tsp lemon juice
Butter Cream Filling (see Extras page 117)

Cream the butter and sugar together until they're light and fluffy, in a food processor if you can. Beat in the eggs one at a time, adding a tablespoon of the flour after each egg. Fold in the rest of the flour, and add the water and lemon juice. Bake in two greased 8" sandwich tins for 20 minutes at 375F. When they're cooled down, fill them with Butter Cream.

pound fruit cake

Ingredients:
1 lb baking flour
10-12 eggs
1 lb butter
1 lb dark sugar
1 tsp nutmeg
1 tsp lime juice
1/8 tsp baking soda
1 tsp vanilla
1 tsp cinnamon
1 tsp lemon rind
2 tbsp browning
1/4 cup rum
1/4 cup port wine
5lbs soaked fruit (see recipe below)

Cream the butter and sugar together in a bowl or food processor. Slowly beat in the eggs, one at a time. Add first the soaked fruits, then the vanilla, nutmeg, cinnamon, lime juice and lemon rind, and the sieved flour. Dissolve the baking soda in a teaspoon of warm water, and add it to the mixture. Bake in two 9" baking tins for 30 minutes at 350F. Then turn the heat down to 250F., and bake for a further 3 1/2 hours. When it's baked, mix the rum and port wine together, evenly pour over the cakes, and let them cool before serving.

soaked fruit:

1 lb raisins
1 lb pitted prunes
1 lb currants
1 lb mixed fruit
1/2 lb pitted dates
1/2 lb figs
1 cup any nuts, finely chopped
1 bottle of rum
1 bottle of port wine

Finely crush the nuts by putting them into a small bag and running a rolling pin over them (or, more simply, using a food processor). Grind all the dry fruit in a meat grinder or food processor. Pour all the alcohol over the fruit and nuts and leave it to marinate for at least 3 months. (Start in June/July for

Christmas). Put it in an airtight jar and it will keep forever. Alternatively, steam the fruit and nuts in the alcohol in a covered sauce pan for 5 minutes. Allow it to cool, and it's ready. Using this method, it will also last forever in an airtight container, reckons Pearl.

g i z z a d a s

"My gizzadas are a little different from anyone else's", says Pearl. "Pearl's gizzadas are the best in the world!",confirms Rita Marley.
Warning—don't forget to let the pastry sit overnight in the refrigerator.

Ingredients:
1 coconut
8 ozs dark brown sugar
10 ozs granulated sugar
1/2 teaspoon nutmeg
1 tsp cinnamon
1/2 rose water
1/2 tsp almond extract
2/3 cup water

Crack open a coconut, and remove the meat with a knife. Grate it by hand; unfortunately, a food processor won't give you the right chunky texture coconut gizzadas need. Bring both kinds of sugar to a boil in the water for 15 minutes, until it forms threads. Add the rose water, almond texture, nutmeg and cinnamon to the mixture. Then add the grated coconut, and cook it over a low heat for 10 minutes, until almost all the liquid has evaporated. Let the mixture cool down, and spoon it into the crust.

pastry
2 cups flour
1/3 cup shortening
2 tsp butter
1 egg
1/4 tsp salt
9 tbsp iced water

With your fingers, mix the flour, shortening, butter, egg, and salt, adding water as needed to make a dough. Refrigerate the dough overnight. Roll the pastry out on a floured board, and cut it into a 5-6 inch circle. To make the pie shell, pinch the edges just like a regular pie crust. Fill with the coconut mixture, and bake at 250F for 20 minutes. You have to check the oven after ten minutes to be sure that the coconut filling hasn't risen over the sides of the pastry. Press it firmly back into its place with a fork if it's getting unruly!

cream pies

(chocolate) rum cream pie

Adding 3 tablespoons of melted chocolate, and 1/2 cup of finely chopped peanuts to this basic rum pie recipe will transform it into a Chocolate Rum Cream Pie, should you so desire.

Ingredients:
3 tbsp melted butter
10 ginger snap biscuits
3 egg yolks
4 dessert spoons sugar
3/4 pack gelatine
1 pint whipped cream
1-2 tbsp white rum
1 tbsp sweet chocolate morsels
Sweet Pie Shell (see Extras page 108)

Whip the egg yolks with the sugar until they're creamy and thick, by hand or with a food processor. Dissolve the gelatine in a tablespoon of hot water, and pour it into the mix, stirring briskly. Set it to cool. Whip the cream until it's stiff, and fold it into the mixture, setting aside a bit for decoration. Add the rum to the mix. Prepare the pie shell using the biscuits/cookies, and pour in the mixture. Decorate the pie with chocolate curls, and whipped cream around the edges. Chill the pie in the fridge until it's firm, and serve cold.

banana coconut pie

Ingredients:
1 cup sugar
juice of one lime
8 baked bananas
1 1/2 cups coconut cream
1 tsp gelatine
1 tsp sweet condensed milk
1 tsp finely chopped nuts
1/4 tsp cinnamon
9"graham cracker pie shell (see Extras page 110)

Peel the bananas, slice them in half lengthwise, sprinkle them with sugar, cinnamon, and lime juice, and bake at 400F for 20 minutes. Let the bananas cool for 10 minutes, then place them in the pie shell. Dissolve half the gelatine in 1 tablespoon of warm water, together with the syrup from the baked bananas, and pour over the bananas. Put it in the fridge to cool for 10 minutes. Dissolve the rest of the gelatine in 1 tablespoon of warm water, with the coconut cream and condensed milk, and pour it over the bananas. Chill in the fridge again for 15 minutes, and serve cold.

chocho pie

The recipe that Pearl ingeniously invented to please her American guest's craving for apple pie during the Jamaican food shortages of the 1970s, when she was running the Boonoonoos Guest House in Runaway Bay.

Ingredients:
3 chochos
2 tsp lime rind
2 tbsp lime juice
2 tsp cornstarch
1/4 cup raisins
1/4 cup brown sugar
1/2 tsp butter
1/2 cup raisins
Sweet Pie Pastry(see Extras page 108)

Peel and slice the chocho as if they were apples, and blanch them by pouring boiling water over them for a few seconds. Lay them evenly around the pastry in an 8" pie dish. Add the sugar, lime rind and juice, and the cinnamon, cornstarch, and raisins. Bake at 350F. for 45 minutes, and serve either hot or cold.

breads

cassava bammy

The hairy cassava root may seem a tough proposition for the uninitiated, but its many uses make it beloved all over the Third World (see Glossary). Not unlike Italian polenta, Jamaican bammy bread is a local institution. It's savoury, filling, and warming —but also, it's convenient. Once prepared, it can be stored in a freezer for up to a week. Right from the freezer, you can either toast or fry it, using these alternative methods. In Jamaica, it's the traditional accompaniment for fried fish. Eat it with lots of pepper.

Ingredients:
2 lbs cassava
1 1/2 tsp salt

Using a very sharp knife, peel and grate the cassava, then wring out the juice in a cheese-cloth or cotton tea towel. Next, push the cassava through a sieve, and mix in the salt. Alas, a food processor cannot be used, as it would ruin the texture. Grease a medium size skillet. Taking a cup of cassava mixture at a time, put it in the skillet, and flatten the 'dough' till it makes a flat cake about 6 inches across. On medium heat, cook the bammy till the edges start to shrink inwards, and the underside of the bammy becomes golden brown, for 5 minutes. Repeat the process till the other side is golden brown too. Carry on making cupfulls of the cassava mix into flat toasted bammy cakes until it's all used up.

To TOAST - Soak the bammy in milk or coconut juice for 2 minutes, and place under the broiler.

To FRY - Soak the bammy in coconut juice or milk for 2 minutes and fry in oil.

banana bread

Ingredients:
5 well ripe bananas
2 eggs
1/2 lb butter
1 cup chopped nuts
1 cup raisins
2 tsp vanilla
4 cups flour
5 tsp baking powder
1 cup sugar
1 tsp nutmeg
pinch of salt

Cream the butter, sugar, and beaten eggs together. Sift the flour, baking powder, nutmeg, and salt into a bowl, then add the nuts and raisins. Mash the bananas by hand or in a food processor, and alternate mixing the mashed banana and the flour mixture into the creamed eggs. Mix it all well together into a sweet dough, mix in the vanilla, and pour the dough into a greased 8 inch baking tin. Bake at 350F. for 1 1/2 hours. This banana bread is delectable hot or cold.

gingerbread deluxe

Ingredients:
3 cups flour
1 tsp baking powder
1 tsp baking soda
1/2 tsp salt
2 tsp ginger
1 tsp cinammon
1/4 tsp nutmeg
1 cup light brown sugar
1/4 cup shortening
1 cup light molasses
1 cup seedless raisins
1 cup water

Sift the flour, baking powder, soda, salt, ginger, cinnamon, and nutmeg together. In another bowl, cream the sugar and shortening until they're fluffy. Dissolve the molasses in a cup of boiling water, and add the raisins. Blend the sugar and molasses mixtures together. Slowly add the new blend to the mix of dry ingredients, stirring well. Grease two 8" loaf tins, and pour the mixture in. Bake at 325F for 40 minutes. Hot or cold, both loaves of gingerbread will be devoured, pronto.

Nutty bun bread

Ingredients:
2 cups flour
1/2 tsp salt
2 tsp baking powder
1/2 cup sugar
1 cup chopped walnuts
1 cup plain yoghurt
1 egg

Sift together the flour, salt, and baking powder, then stir in the sugar and chopped walnuts. In another bowl, beat the eggs well, and stir in the yoghurt. Add the egg mixture to the dry ingredients, and mix well. Put the dough in a greased loaf tin, and let it stand for 30 minutes to rise. Bake at 375F. for 45-50 minutes, and serve hot or cold.

∫weet potato buN

Many Americans mistake the red-skinned sweet potato for a yam. Don't be fooled.

Ingredients:
1 cup of mashed cooked sweet potato(1/2 lb. sweet potatoes)
2 cups flour
4 tbsps baking powder
1/2 tsp baking soda
1/4 tsp cinnamon
1/4 tsp vanilla
1/2 cup milk
1 egg
1/2 tsp salt
1 tbsp butter or margarine
1/2 cup brown sugar

Peel the sweet potatoes, boil for 15 minutes till soft, then mash in a bowl. Warm the milk, and mix it with the butter in a bowl. In another bowl, lightly beat together the egg, cinnamon, vanilla, sugar, and salt. Mix everything together into one bowl, and add the mashed cooked sweet potato. Add the flour, baking powder, and soda, and mix it all into a firm dough. Shape it into a roll, put it on a greased baking dish, and bake at 375F. for 30 minutes. This sweet bun can be served hot or cold.

jamaica spiced bun

This rich, fruity, spicy bun is an archetype of Jamaican baking, and a perennial favourite.It's formally eaten with a hard cheese as an Easter treat.

Ingredients:
1 pack of active dry yeast / 1 yeast cake
1 tsp nutmeg
1 egg
1/2 pint milk
1/2 lb butter
1 cup brown sugar
1 tbs. molasses
8 cups flour
1 cup water
1 tsp salt
1/4 lb crystallised cherries
1/4 lb currants
1/4 lb chopped raisins
1/4 chopped lemon
1 tsp cinnamon
pinch of mixed spice
1 tsp caraway seeds
1 tsp anise seed
For the Glaze:
1 cup sugar
3 tbsp water
3 tbsp butter

Dissolve the yeast in lukewarm water. Scald the milk, and boil the water, and pour them together. Put the butter, sugar, salt, and all the spices in a bowl, and pour the milk and water mixture over them. Beat the eggs, and add them to the mix, with the anise seed. Sieve half the flour into the mixture, and stir well. Stir in the yeast, and add the fruits to the mixture. Add enough flour to make a stiff dough. Cover the mixing bowl, and let the mixture rise till it's doubled in size. Knead the dough, and mix in the rest of the flour. Knead it well once more. Shape the dough into loaves, and put it into four 8" greased loaf tins. Bake at 350F. for 1 hour, until the buns shrink back from the sides of the tins. Before they're cold, you can glaze the buns by boiling the ingredients specified above, then brushing the glaze on top of the loaves.

Perhaps the most versatile of any chapter in this book, the goodies in "Extras" are adaptable to all your cooking cravings.

pastries and pie crusts

potato pie crust

Ingredients:
2 cups cold mashed potatoes (ideal for leftovers)
1/4 tsp salt
1/4 cup milk
1 1/2 tsp baking powder
1 cup flour
1 oz butter

Mix the mashed potatoes with the flour, salt, and baking powder in a bowl. Slowly add enough milk to make a dough that's light and soft, but still dry. Fold in 1/3 of the butter, and roll the dough out again. Repeat the process until all the butter is used up, then roll the potato crust out and cover the pie before baking.

sweet or savoury pie shell

Ingredients:
2 1/2-3 cups all purpose flour
1 tbsp sugar (if making sweet pie shell)
1 tsp salt
1 cup shortening
2 tbsp butter or margarine
7-8 tbsp cold water

Sieve the flour and salt into a large mixing bowl, and cut in the shortening. Add the sugar if making the sweet pie shell. Sprinkle in the water, one tablespoon at a time. Mix all the ingredients together into a dough. Flour the pastry board, and the rolling pin, and roll the pastry out to the appropriate size.

s p i N N e r s   d u M p L i N g s

Ingredients:
1 1/2 cups plain flour
1/2 tsp salt
water

Mix the flour and salt together in a big bowl. Little by little, add the water ro make a dough. Break the dough into small pieces, and roll it into balls shaped like a slender cigar, about 3-4 inches long and 1/2" at their widest point. Boil in water, or in the soup, for 15-20 minutes. This recipe makes 12 dumplings.

r i c e   c r u s t

Ingredients:
1 cup cold boiled rice
1 tbsp melted butter
1/2 cup milk
1 tsp baking powder
1/2 tsp salt
1/2 cup flour
2 eggs

Separate the egg yolk and whites. Mix the rice, milk, and the beaten egg yolks into a bowl, and sift the salt and baking powder into it. Melt the butter, and mix it well in. Beat the egg whites stiffly, and fold them in. Pour the crust mixture over any filling—fish, meat or vegetables.

patty pastry

Ingredients:
3 cups flour
1/2 lb suet
1 level tsp salt
2 tsp baking powder

Mix all the ingredients together into a bowl. Add enough water to make a dough. Flour the rolling board and pin for smooth rolling, then form the dough into a ball, and gently roll it. Using a saucer as a guide, cut circles out of the pastry for the patties. Place 1 tbsp of meat, or ackees, in the centre of each circle, fold the edges over the 'spine' of the patty, and seal the edge by crimping with a fork. Use a little milk to baste the edges to ensure good sealing, if you like. Cook as the recipe says — a general guide is 350F for 30 minutes. You can eat patties hot or cold.

graham cracker pie shell

Any dry crackers can be used. This pie shell is suitable for any sweet pie.

Ingredients:
1 1/2 cups crushed graham crackers
1 tsp flour
2 tbsp sugar
1/4 cup melted butter

Mix everything together in a bowl. Grease an 8" pie dish, and press the mixture firmly and evenly all over the sides and bottom of the dish. Bake at 350F for 10 minutes, then cool the shell in the fridge for 30 minutes. Pour the pie contents into the shell, and you're ready to eat.

gingersnap pie shells

A sweet and spicy pie shell. These quantities are suitable for a Rum Cream Pie.

Ingredients:
3 tbsp melted butter
10 gingersnap biscuits

Melt the butter in a saucepan on low heat. Crush the biscuits, and stir them together with the melted butter in a bowl, till they're mixed into a paste. Grease a pie dish, and making sure that there are no holes anywhere, cover the sides and bottom of the dish with the gingersnap mixture. Scallop the edges of the pastry with your thumb and forefinger into a pretty pattern, and let the pie shell chill in the fridge for 5 minutes before putting the pie contents into the shell.

sauces and gravies

curry sauce

Ingredients:
1 tbsp margarine
1 onion
2 tbsp curry
1 apple
1 hot pepper
2 cups chicken/beef/vegetable stock

Heat a skillet and put in the margarine. Chop the onion, apple, and hot pepper, and throw them in the skillet together with the curry powder, salt and pepper. Mix them up together, and cook on a high gas for 3 minutes. Add the stock, and cook for a further 5-10 minutes on medium to low heat.

LeMON butter Sauce

Ingredients:
1/2 cup butter
2 tbsp lemon juice
1 tbsp chopped parsley
1/4 tsp chopped hot pepper

Heat the butter, and add the lemon juice when it's melted. Add the chopped parsley and hot pepper, and it's ready to serve.

ruM butter Sauce

Ingredients:
4 ozs butter
1/2 cup icing sugar
1/4 cup rum

Combine all the ingredients in a bowl and place in the fridge. It takes about 1 1/2 hours for the Rum Butter Sauce to get appropriately hard. In a sealed container it keeps for a year when frozen, six months when refrigerated.

cheese Sauce

Ingredients:
1 tbsp butter or margarine
1 tbsp flour
1/4 tsp salt
1/8 tsp white pepper
1 1/2 cups of milk
1/2 cup grated cheese

Mix the flour and butter in a saucepan on a low heat until they're well blended. Add salt and pepper, and cook for three minutes. Remove the saucepan from the heat, and slowly add the milk, mixing well until it's a smooth thick liquid. Return the saucepan to the heat, stirring constantly. Add the cheese, and cook for 5 minutes, stirring, until it's blended into the liquid..

seafood sauce

This is particularly good with fritters.

Ingredients:
3 tbsp ketchup
2 tbsp mayonnaise
1 tsp pepper mustard
1 chilli pepper (optional)
Mix all the ingredients together in a bowl or mixer until they're smooth. Add the finely chopped chilli pepper, if you like it hot.

rich thick cream sauce

Ingredients:
1/2 cup butter or margarine
1/2 cup flour
1/2 cup cream
1/2 cup milk
salt and pepper
Melt the butter in a saucepan on a low heat. Mix in the flour, salt, and pepper, until it's as smooth as possible. Remove the saucepan from the heat, and slowly stir in the milk and cream. Bring it to the boil, stirring. This should take about two minutes.

hot sauce

Ingredients:
1/2 cup tomato ketchup
1 tsp tabasco sauce/bottled hot sauce
1/4 tsp mustard
Mix all the ingredients together until they've become a thick, creamy sauce.

White Sauce

Ingredients:
1 tbsp butter or margarine
1 tbsp flour
1/4 tsp salt
1/8 tsp white pepper
1 1/2 cups milk

Melt the butter in a saucepan. Add the flour, salt, and pepper, and cook on a low heat, stirring until all the flour is absorbed in the butter. Remove the saucepan from the heat and stir in the milk. Put the saucepan back on the heat, bring to the boil, and stir continually until the sauce is smooth and all the lumps are dissolved. This usually takes about 2 minutes.

Sweet and Sour Sauce

Ingredients:
1 1/2 tbsp any oil
2 cloves garlic
1/2 medium pineapple finely chopped/tin of pineapple finely chopped
1 tbsp finely chopped ginger
1 1/2 tbsp vinegar
1 1/2tbsp brown sugar
2 tbsp cornstarch
2 tsp dry sherry (optional)
2 tsp soy sauce
3/4 pint water
1 stalk finely chopped spring onion for a garnish

Heat the oil in a saucepan and add the garlic, pineapple, and ginger, and cook for 2 minutes. Mix together in a bowl the vinegar, sugar, cornstarch, soy sauce, water, and sherry (if you're using it.) Pour the soy sauce mixture into the pineapple mixture, stirring. Just before serving, chop the spring onion, and use it for decoration.

MUSHROOM SAUCE

Ingredients:
10 mushrooms
1/2 onion
1 tbsp butter or margarine
1 tsp worcestershire sauce
1 tsp pickapeppa sauce
1 tsp gravy browning
3 tsps cornstarch
1 cup chicken/beef broth
salt and pepper

Melt the butter or margarine in a saucepan on medium heat. Finely chop the onions and mushrooms, and add them to the saucepan with the pickapeppa and worcestershire sauces, and the gravy browning. Cook for 1 minute. Add the broth and cook for a minute more, then thicken with 1-3 level teaspoons of cornstarch, depending on how thick you want your sauce.

BROWN GRAVY

Ingredients:
2 tsps cornstarch
2 ozs butter
1 cup chicken/meat stock
1 onion/2 scallions
1 tsp soy sauce
1 tbsp worcestershire sauce

Melt the butter in a skillet, and add the cornstarch. Stir in the stock until it's smooth. Add the chopped onions, the soy sauce, and the worcester sauce, stir it all in together, and let the sauce cook into a thick gravy. This should take 10-15 minutes.

salad dressings

Avocado dressing

Ingredients:
1 ripe avocado
1/4 cup lemon/lime juice
1 small onion
1/2 cup olive oil
salt and pepper
Mash the avocado, and mix it with all the ingredients, by hand in a bowl, or in a mixer.

tangy pepper dressing

This dressing goes with either a salad, or a savoury dish.

Ingredients:
1 small bottle mustard
12 chilli peppers
1 large onion
1/4 cup vinegar
1 tsp allspice
Chop the chilli peppers and onion, and blend all the ingredients together either in a blender, or by hand in a bowl. Chill in the refrigerator for about 1 hour.

garlic dressing

Ingredients:
1/2 cup olive oil
1/3 cup vinegar or lemon juice
1 tsp mustard
1-5 cloves of garlic, to taste

1 tsp sugar
salt and pepper

Crush the garlic, and mix everything together either by hand in a bowl, or in a mixer, until it's thick and creamy.

cake creams

butter cream

Ingredients:
3 ozs butter
8 ozs icing sugar
1 tbsp rum
1 tbsp orange juice
1 tbsp orange rind

Mix everything together by hand in a bowl, or in a mixer. Use the butter cream as a sandwich filling between two cake halves, and frost the top with icing sugar.

Honey butter cream

Ingredients:
2 ozs butter
6 ozs icing sugar
2 tbsp honey
1/4 cup ground almonds

Mix everything together by hand in a bowl, or in a mixer. Spread half the mixture as a sandwich filling on the bottom cake layer, placing the other cake half on top of it. Then spread the remaining honey butter cream over the top of the combined cakes. Sprinkle icing sugar on top of the honey butter cream on the upper layer of cake.

coconuts

coconut water

Coconut water is the liquid you get by cracking open a coconut, and pouring out the "water" within. It's both a healthy, nutritious drink on its own, and a great addition to recipes, or more complex blended drinks.

coconut juice

Ingredients:
The white meat of 1 small coconut
3 cups water
Break the coconut meat into small pieces, and blend it with the water until it's smooth. You may need to do this in batches. The juice is used in both cooking and baking.

coconut cream

Once the coconut milk has been squeezed from the meat of the coconut, the residue—what they call 'trash' in Jamaica—can be re-cycled into pastry for baking. As Pearl proudly points out, "The only bit of coconut we don't use in cooking is the shell". Coconut cream is often eaten in Jamaica with a simply steamed guava, or plainly baked pineapple or banana.

Ingredients:
7 dry coconuts
1 tsp gelatine
2 tsps. condensed milk/sugar (optional)
Crack open the coconut, and remove the white coconut flesh from the shell, using a knife. Make sure that all the brown skin encasing the white meat is completely cleaned. Grate the coconut, either by hand, or in a food processor after cutting it into small pieces. Squeeze the coconut milk from the coconut by pushing it through a clean cheese cloth, or cotton tea towel. Dissolve the gelatine in a little warm water, and stir it into the coconut milk. Grease a six inch mold with vegetable oil, and pour the coconut cream into it. Put it into a refrigerator for 2-3 hours. Turn the coconut cream out onto a platter, and it's ready to accompany any of the recommended dishes.

drinks

cool

Naturally, life in the tropics has made Pearl a mistress of the cool, invigorating drink. Here's some crucial thirst quenchers, poured straight from Bell's blender.
The method for making all these drinks is simple: Put all the ingredients into a blender with ice, and serve (unless otherwise stated).

MATRIMONY

Ingredients:
6 star apples
6 oranges
1/4 cup sugar (optional)
Wash the star apples and slice off their tops. Taking out the pulp, scoop out the seeds. Peel and core the oranges, and take out the meat of the fruit from its skin. Mash the star apple and orange together, add sugar if you so desire, and chill before serving.
Serves 6

family fruit drink

Peel and dice all the fruits into small pieces before blending.

Ingredients:
2 cups orange juice
1 ripe banana
1 ripe mango
1 apple
1 peach
2 slices pineapple
1 pint vanilla ice cream
1 slice paw-paw/papaya

mothers day delight

Serve this with a slice of orange and a cherry as decoration.

Ingredients:
1/2 cup rum/Irish Cream liqueur
1/2 cup fresh orange juice
3 fresh cherries
3 slices of orange
Serves 2-3

grandfathers drink:

Ingredients:
1/2 cup orange juice
1/2 cup whisky
1/2 cup pineapple
1/4 cup brandy
Serves 3-4

grandmothers drink

Ingredients:
1 tbsp Courvoisier liqueur (optional)
1/2 cup hot coffee
1/4 cup whipped cream
1/4 cup Cointreau liqueur
Add the Cointreau to the hot coffee, and top with whipped cream. The Courvoisier adds color.
Serves 3-4

After dinner drink

Ingredients:
2/3 cup cold coffee
1/4 cup rum/Irish Cream liqueur
1/4 cup Cointreau
1 tbsp clear syrup
5 tbsp cream
Serves 2

carrorange juice

Cut the carrots into 1 inch slices,put them into the juicer, and make sure they're thoroughly blended into a liquid. Don't put ice in the blender, but chill before serving. Pearl says, "It's so filling that it's the perfect nutritional breakfast for dieters".

Ingredients:
2 cups orange juice
3 medium carrots
Serves 2

banana daiquiri

Peel the bananas before blending! As well as putting ice in the blender, chill till ice cold before serving.

Ingredients:
3 ripe bananas
1/2 cup lime juice
1/2 cup rum
1/2 cup syrup
Serves 3-4

New Years Morning drink

A power-packed pick-me-up when you need it most.

Ingredients:
2 cups milk
1/2 cup rum or whisky
1 tbsp sugar
1/8 tsp nutmeg
1 egg
2 drops almond extract
dash of bitters
Serves 4

Naseberry or kiwi daiquiri

Peel the naseberries or kiwis and remove all the seeds before serving. Peel the kiwis, if you're using them. Garnish with the orange slices and cherries.
NB: no ice unless desired.

Ingredients:
3 naseberries/kiwis
1 cup orange juice
1 tsp sugar
1/2 cup rum
3-4 cherries
3-4 orange slices

pumpkin punch

Decorate with the mint, and chill before serving.

Ingredients:
1 cup cooked mashed pumpkin
1 pint milk
1/2 tsp vanilla
1/4 tsp nutmeg
1/4 cup brandy or rum
1/2 tin condensed milk
a few sprigs of mint
Serves 4-6

soursop drink

Ingredients:
1 large well ripe soursop
1/2 cup sugar
1 tbsp lime juice
1/8 tsp nutmeg
1 tbsp lime juice
condensed milk to taste (optional)
pinch of salt

Peel the soursop, and rub the fruit through a sieve into a jug. Add the lime juice, nutmeg, salt, and sugar, and mix it all up together. If you've got a sweet tooth, you can add condensed milk, but then you must omit the lime juice. Serve with crushed ice.

sea grape drink

Blend the sea grapes first, in a short burst, so that the seeds remain for extra texture. Add all the other ingredients next, blending briefly once more. Don't use ice — just chill till the drink's cold.

Ingredients:
1 quart ripe sea grapes
5 cups water
1/4 cup lime juice
sugar to taste
1/4 cup rum (optional)

mint cocktail

Ingredients:
1 pint boiling water
2 branches black mint
juice of 1 orange
2 bottles of 7 Up
juice of 1 lime
1/2 cup granulated sugar
4-6 fresh cherries
4-6 slices of orange
some sprigs of mint

Pour the boiling water over the black mint, and leave it to stand for five minutes. Strain the water, and add sugar, before chilling in the fridge for 30 minutes, or longer if possible. Then add the orange and lime juice, and the 7 Up. Serve with ice cubes, adding the orange slices, the cherries and some fresh sprigs of mint as garnish.
Serves 4-6

Lemon fizz

Ingredients:
1/2 cup sugar
1 pint water
1/4 cup lime juice
2 cups soda water
Mix together the sugar water and lime juice, and finally, the soda water. Serve with ice cubes.
Serves 4-6

pineapple drink

Ingredients:
1 pineapple skin
1 quart boiling water
1 one inch piece of ginger root
sugar to taste
Pour the boiling water over the pineapple skins, and add the grated ginger root. Let the mixture sit for 6-8 hours, and chill before serving, adding sugar if you like sweet things.(Like Pearl.)
Serves 4-6

potato punch

A nice thick drink that everyone thinks is an ice cream milk shake, says Pearl.
Ingredients:
2 large cooked potatoes
1 pint milk
1/2 tin condensed milk
1/2 tsp vanilla
1/4 tsp nutmeg
Serves 4-5

tutti frutti

Ingredients:
1 ripe banana
1 apple
1 peach
1 pear
1 cup orange juice
1 cup grapefruit juice
2 slices pineapple
2 naseberries
juice of 1 lime
1/2 cup strawberries
1 mango
1 cup strawberry syrup
3-4 cherries
3-4 orange slices

Peel and remove the skins from all the fruit, and blend at high speed. Chill for about an hour in the deep freeze before serving, garnished with orange slices and cherries.
Serves 3-4

egg Nog carrot drink

Chill before serving

Ingredients:
2 eggs
4 cups carrot juice
1/2 cup sugar
1/2 tsp nutmeg
1/2 cup rum or brandy (optional)

glossary

ackee

They say that the mysterious ackee was brought to Jamaica from West Africa by the infamous Captain Bligh aboard his ship, the Bounty, in 1787. Since then, the ackee has occupied a unique place at the heart of Jamaican food lore. There's a poetry to its very growth that adds mystique to its dainty texture and taste, and its creamy, scrambled-egg appearance. The tree grows pretty, fragrant white flowers, and the ackee itself — a bulbous, leathery orange-red fruit, which bursts apart when ripe to reveal shiny black seeds, their stems encased in the primrose yellow ackee meat, properly known as an aril. Here is where the trouble begins, for if the ackee is force-ripened, or if all the red veins are not removed from the aril in cleaning, the ackee can be fatally poisonous. Deaths from eating ackee are not infrequently reported in the Jamaican press. However, it remains a major island delicacy, its classic preparation being ackee and saltfish. But vegetarians can find many uses for the nutty, slightly-sweet, sensuous consistency of the delicious ackee. Outside Jamaica, the tinned and freeze-dried varieties must suffice, as the ackee tree scarcely grows off the island.

banana

It is one of nature's amusing tricks that the banana is not the fruit of a tree, though it looks just like it. The banana tree is actually an enormous herbaceous grass plant. Categories aside, the banana has contributed enormously to the Jamaican economy, and equally to its menus. There's a rich variety of bananas — the familiar 'ripe' banana, commonly eaten as a fruit internationally, and the dainty, petite 'sweety' bananas. Then there's the cooking kind: the hefty scimitar of plantains, and the unripe green banana, commonly eaten as a starchy vegetable. Before boiling green bananas, don't remove the skin, but top and tail it with a knife, and slash slices along it to facilitate its removal when boiled.

callaloo

The slightly tart, spinach-like green leaf of the taro plant, also known as dasheen, is also beloved as a soup. Outside Jamaica, it can be found in West Indian markets, or canned.

cassava

A staple starchy root vegetable throughout the tropics, legend has it that Italian adventurer Christopher Columbus ate it at dinner with the king of the cannibal Carib tribe on December 26, 1492. The Arawak Indians are reputed to have first discovered how to remove the prussic acid that can make Cassava poisonous; they would bite into raw cassav and commit suicide rather than face torture from the Spanish invaders. Nowadays, the cassava root is an integral part of Jamaican dishes such as Bammy Bread, and Pepperpot Soup.

cho-cho
(christophine/coyote squash)

The central ingredient of Pearl's Cho-Cho Pie originally originated in Mexico, and arrived in Jamaica in the 18th century. It's a pear-shaped squash or gourd, with a hard green skin, and white to light green flesh around a central heart , which can be eaten. When boiled, it tastes not unlike a courgette or marrow.

conch

The conch shell has a history as distinguished as its glossy visual appeal. The Maroons, the escaped slaves of Jamaica, used it as a horn (the Abeng,) to summon friends in revolt, and warn of foes. The conch fish, an offshoot of the snail family, is a favourite of Pearl Bell's; although it's labour intensive, it's strong taste and texture are unique. There are no short cuts to preparing conch, but it's a good thing to do to release pent-up aggression. You take the conch from the shell, carefully remove all the red veins, and then simply beat it, thwack it, and hit it, with a mallet or similar heavy object, until it's thoroughly tenderised. Alternatively, enlightened fish shops sell it prepared, or it can be found canned.

eggplant (garden egg/aubergine)

A favourite of international cuisines, all over the Middle East, in Greece, and across the Caribbean, the eggplant is part of the potato family, though you'd never guess it from its shiny dark purple skin. It's common to sprinkle salt all over the sliced eggplant, and leave it to stand for a few minutes before washing off the bitter juices it sweats out.

naseberry (sapodilla)

The white flowers and leathery oval leaves of the naseberry tree surround a fruit that's particularly prized for use in drinks, custards, and even ice cream, as well as eating on its own or in a fruit salad.. Peel the cafe-au-lait coloured skin of the naseberry, remove the seeds, and use the fleshy pulp. Make sure you pick a soft naseberry, as they're bitter when under ripe. The sap of the tree trunk is used in the manufacture of chewing gum.

okra (lady's finger)

Africans, Jamaicans, Indians, and Middle Easterners prize the 'gummy' texture of okra, which seems simply slimey to unaccustomed Western palates. It's a taste worth acquiring. It grows as a pod-like fruit just beneath a pretty pale yellow flower, and surprisingly belongs to the same family as the vibrantly colored hibiscus flower. It's 'slime' is useful for thickening soups and stews, or it can be par-boiled before adding it to other elements in a stew. Equally, you can just boil it, eat it, and enjoy it, 'slime' and all.

paw paw (papaya)

The subtle red-orange flesh of the paw paw is a common breakfast food, eaten like a slice of melon with lime squeezed over it. Chrstopher Columbus' Journals note that the natives of the Caribbean islands were very strong, and mostly ate a tree melon called 'the fruit of angels'. He meant the paw paw. It's health giving qualities derive from a protein-digesting enzyme, papain, found in both the leaves and the fruit, which can even tenderize meat that's wrapped in the leaves.

PLANTAIN (see bANANA)

SALTfISH

Cod is the fish that responds best to being preserved in salt, and salted codfish is a staple of many creative cuisines that have refined the foodstuffs of poverty and hardship into delicacies. Saltfish was the staple food of slavery. That is, slaves were bought with saltfish used as currency, and the luckier slaves were fed saltfish. It's a food designed for storage on long sea journeys, and it's just as convenient in your kitchen cupboard. The 'proper' preparation involves soaking overnight in cold water, then putting it in a saucepan of cold water, boiling it, and letting it simmer for 15 minutes before skinning and flaking it. If you haven't got the time, just wash it in several changes of cold water, quickly boil it, then drain before skinning and flaking.

sea grape

The pretty heart-shaped leaves of the sea grape tree, with their prominent red veins grows as a shrub by the sea, and as a tree inland. The fruit is too sour to eat raw, but is delicious when prepared in a drink as Pearl reccomends.

soursop

Looking like an overgrown, warty avocado, the soursop was originally a native of South America. The sweet, slightly tart soursop flesh is mousse-like, a pale, pale baby pink, with a dulcet taste. It's popularly used in drinks, ice creams, and sorbets.

STAR Apple

The star apple's plain purple skin conceals a fetchingly graphic interior, with the star of its name clearly visible in brown stripes through the pink and white flesh. It tastes like an insant sorbet, slightly crunchy, with a delicate sweetness.

YAM

The yam is an eternal fixture in Caribbean food. Its brown bulk is slightly hairy — not the most glamorous looking of vegetables, the utilitarian appearance of this root tuber is matched by its usefulness in everyday Caribbean food. Like the adaptable potato, it can be roasted, baked, fried, boiled, mashed — it's an infinitely adaptable starch staple.

index